Educational Leadership at 2050

Conjectures, Challenges, and Promises

Fenwick W. English, Rosemary Papa, Carol A. Mullen, and Ted Creighton

ROWMAN & LITTLEFIELD EDUCATION
A division of
ROWMAN & LITTLEFIELD PUBLISHERS, INC.
Lanham • New York • Toronto • Plymouth, UK

Published by Rowman & Littlefield Education
A division of Rowman & Littlefield Publishers, Inc.
A wholly owned subsidary of The Rowman & Littlefield Publishing Group, Inc.
4501 Forbes Boulevard, Suite 200, Lanham, Maryland 20706
http://www.rowman.com

10 Thornbury Road, Plymouth PL6 7PP, United Kingdom

British Library Cataloguing in Publication Information Available

Library of Congress Cataloging-in-Publication Data

Educational leadership at 2050 : conjectures, challenges, and promises / Fenwick W. English ... [et al.].
  p. cm.
Includes bibliographical references.
ISBN 978-1-61048-794-8 (cloth : alk. paper) — ISBN 978-1-61048-795-5 (pbk. : alk. paper) — ISBN 978-1-61048-796-2 (electronic)
1. Educational leadership—United States. 2. School management and organization—United States. I. English, Fenwick W.
LB2805.E34754 2012
371.2'011—dc23
2011049051

Printed in the United States of America

Contents

Foreword

A Continuing Conversation: Educational Administration Programming as an Instrument for Educational Reform

James Berry

Improvement of education was an admonition that was hung on educational administration going back to the founding of the profession in the early 1900s and was manifested in the great success of educational bureaucracy in the twentieth century. From the first decade of the twentieth century to the first decade of the twenty-first century, educational administration rode the wave of improvement and success. As schooling in the United States expanded, so did programs of preparation. Although the field enjoyed growth and expansion, there were always questions about an appropriate curriculum for the preparation of school leaders, the proper approach to instruction, and the quality of programs.

Hackmann and McCarthy (2011) described educational administration as being "at a crossroads" in the United States (p. 269). They noted that programs of preparation "face increasing external pressures as states contemplate reducing or eliminating licensure requirements for school leaders. The virtual monopoly that universities enjoyed in providing leadership preparation is no longer assured" (p. 269).

The pressures to change are real, yet programs of preparation have been largely standing at this crossroad for forty years. This publication, the thoughtful work of a special task force of scholar-practitioners, represents a continuing effort to undertake some substantive and necessary changes by candidly examining the external and internal forces of our times.

The founding of the National Council of Professors of Educational Administration (NCPEA) is directly linked to the need for understanding and communicating how to better prepare educational leaders.

At the first meeting of professors of educational administration on March 2, 1947, "Ward Miller, Paul R. Mort, John Bracken, and E. T. Peterson were the four panel speakers who led the group into and through a discussion of their problems in preparing school administrators and the methods they were using to try to meet such problems" (Flesher & Knoblauch, 1957, p. ix). The problems of preparation at this meeting in 1947 have continued as a professional topic for over sixty years.

English, Papa, Mullen, and Creighton carry this conversation into the twenty-first century by focusing on the same issues that drove these professors to found NCPEA: How can the profession "achieve a better understanding of the problems of developing educational leaders" and "bring about a common approach regarding the methods and techniques for the more effective preparation of educational administrators" (p. 2)?

THE RISE OF AMERICAN EDUCATION

For the first seventy years of educational administration preparation in the twentieth century, the curriculum was shaped by the bureaucratic nature of K–12 schooling. Bureaucracy, however, was more than an approach to managing a public school district. Bu-reaucracy in education meant a management approach that shaped teaching and learning as an extension of its industrial origins.

The twentieth-century educational administration curriculum was taught by professors who espoused the management and effi-ciency of large-scale school systems in the same way industrial titans promoted the advantages of bureaucratic efficiency, top-down leadership, and economy of scale. Professors of educational administration delivered on a training that enhanced management skill, efficiency of operation, fiscal restraint, and bureaucratic deci-sion-making.

One can track the success of the field of educational administra-tion just by following the arc of twentieth-century American indus-trial prowess. *The Organization Man* (Whyte, 1956) was as much a description of the school leader as of the business manager who took "the vows of organization life" (p. 3). *The Principles of Scien-tific Management*, written by Taylor in 1911, was as important for shaping market-driven values and beliefs in industry as it was for outlining managerial hierarchy and labor efficiency in education.

It was in the power of the ideas—including standardization, effi-ciency, unit cost, time and motion studies to determine labor rates, leadership by well-bred men (rather than qualified men)—that the educational archetype arose and came to dominate the late twenti-eth-century ideal of modern education, modern schooling, and modern educational leadership.

It was not just business that bred the archetypal organization man. The *educational organization man and woman* arose, and were embraced, celebrated, and honored throughout the twentieth century when public education modeled itself after business. The one best educational system Tyack described (1974) was an exten-sion of business. Professors of educational administration worked hand in hand with industrial managers as they educated school managers to run their schools more like factories.

During the twentieth century professors in the field of educational administration trained aspiring educational leaders to manage an expanding educational enterprise that went from rural to suburban, small to large, organizationally simple to organizationally complex.

These same professors embraced business practices and advocated for scientific management as education in the United States was transformed into the larger, more centralized and bureaucratically arranged school districts that emerged out of small agrarian communities. Educational administration programs grew from one formal program at Columbia University in 1905 to over 590 in 2008 (Hackmann & McCarthy, 2011, p. 276).

Throughout the twentieth century the field of educational administration developed a knowledge base about what a school leader should know and do as a practicing leader. The curriculum for educational administration preparation was grounded in practical, professional, and academic knowledge that represented a mix of good old American know-how and common sense, knowledge of the modern world, and study of the theories and principles of leading and managing.

Quality education was equated with standardization of operation, routine, and low cost. Engelhardt (1931), who authored *Public School Organization and Administration*, wrote:

> The application of the scientific method to education has made it possible for school officials to investigate the practices and procedures followed in carrying on school work, and to select from among the activities performed those which should be routinized and for which standard practices might well be devised. For example, standardized intelligence, achievement, and instructional tests which have been developed have contributed in no small way to the improvement of instruction in providing objective measures for the evaluation of the classroom work. (p. 140)

Chamberlain and Kindred (1949) summarized an effective school district at mid-century as "a unit that is large enough to reduce as much as possible inequalities in tax burdens and educational opportunities, to provide capable leadership on boards of education and in the office of the superintendent, to place the appointment of every teacher and the direction of every school in the hands of a trained school executive, and to make possible schools of effective and economical size" (p. 98).

During the twentieth century, on the shoulders of professors of educational administration, the system was outlined, defined, and refined. Programs in educational administration were committed to preparing educational organization men and women who excelled at developing a thorough and efficient system of education.

ORGANIZING FOR LEARNING IN 2050

The twenty-first-century educational system is but an extension of the bureaucratically arranged system of the twentieth century. Efforts of educational reform that emerged in the late 1960s and 1970s, notably under the rubric of the effective schools movement, had a limited impact on the core technology of teaching and learning in US schools.

Although there have been significant attempts to transform schools and school districts through school improvement, the lasting effect of the past forty years of educational reform remains a largely unfulfilled effort to identify agreed-upon educational practices that advance student learning.

The authors of *Educational Leadership at 2050: Conjectures, Challenges, and Promises* make the case that programming in educational administration (1) is an instrument of reform and (2) there are structural components that have to be built into the curriculum of twenty-first-century educational leadership preparation programs. To have a meaningful impact on learning in schools in the United States, leadership preparation programs need to revisit the content, delivery, and focus of leading for learning.

FOCUS REFORM ON TEACHING AND LEARNING

There is a growing clarity that building educational administration programs around a structure(s) that creates the conditions for learning is a more important foundation for leadership than managerial efficiency, bureaucratic expediency, and student and adult accountability. Unless educational administration programs address the core technology of education—teaching and learning—there will continue to be questions about a curriculum that is grounded in the dated ideas and principles of industrial management.

As Wayne Gretzky anticipated the puck, educational administration must anticipate the future. Central to any leadership curriculum must be an understanding of how to improve learning outcomes for all children. Efforts to improve educational administration programs must begin with, and emphasize, teaching and learning as the core technology of educational leadership.

BUREAUCRACY AS REFORM

The most potent reform instrument of the past one hundred years has been the organizational structure of the US school system. It shaped learning within the bureaucratic and economic model that emerged during the Industrial Revolution in the United States and continues its hold on teaching and learning by its very nature as a successful centralized, hierarchically controlling, bureaucratically arranged, and economically efficient model for educating the masses.

It is exactly what the nation wanted and needed during the twentieth century. It is, in the twenty-first century, an instrument of great power. Yet its usefulness as an instrument of educational reform needs to be recast in the twenty-first century.

TECHNOLOGY AS AN ORGANIZING STRUCTURE FOR EDUCATIONAL ADMINISTRATION

The bureaucratically arranged school system is not going away, but it is about to go through a transformation that will shape learning throughout the twenty-first century. Educational administration must lead the development of a learning environment constructed within a virtual bureaucracy. It will be built on the foundation of twentieth-century education that has met twenty-first century learning technology.

The educational organization is about to become a hybrid learning system of bricks *and* clicks. The educational administration professor must anticipate the future of teaching, leading, and learning in a bureaucratically arranged virtual system that one can hardly imagine.

The educational leader of the future will require skills that are only now becoming evident, in a school system that is only now beginning to emerge. The educational administration program must become an early adopter of an altogether different approach to teaching and learning if it is to remain relevant in the face of accelerating change.

> Faculty currently in leadership preparation programs can simply try to keep up with and respond to the rapid technological advances in the external environment, or they can be at the forefront in anticipating issues that need to be addressed in a thoughtful manner. (Hackmann & McCarthy, 2011, p. 284)

The educational administration program of the future reflects a time- and place-bound, bureaucratically organized system that is complemented by a digital structure built on the Internet. Within this emerging bureaucratic system, an enhanced form of virtual teaching and virtual learning will take its place as a mainstream form of learning (see figure F.1).

The technological advance of learning is in its infancy. There is much we do not know. Yet it is evident that programs of preparation will need to adjust to the pedagogy of technology in a classroom and within the virtual bureaucracy.

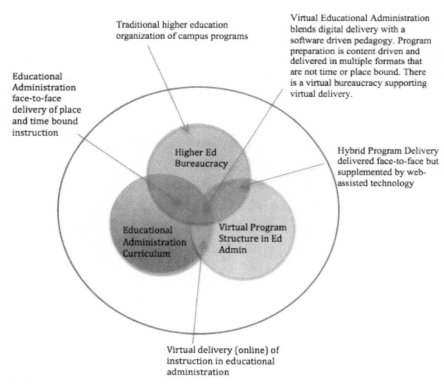

Figure F.1

SUMMARY: TOWARD PEDAGOGICALLY CENTERED LEADERSHIP

This text is one in a continuing line of books, monographs, and papers that take a snapshot and then suggest improvements in the training of leaders for US schools (see, for example, Campbell & Newell, 1973; Griffiths et al., 1988; Murphy, 1992; McCarthy & Kuh, 1997; Hackmann & McCarthy, 2011). It is hoped that this book will be used as a guide to advance the conversation—started within the field of educational administration in 1947—and to help develop a curriculum that builds upon what we already know about school leadership.

The authors make the point that preparation programs should uncouple the *role* of educational leader from the *responsibility* of an educational leader in revising the educational leadership curriculum. For forty years educational administration has advocated training principals, superintendents, and K–12 leaders for positions as instructional leaders.

The authors likewise propose that *pedagogically centered leadership* is a performance-based requirement that clearly communicates—to the education profession, business community, parents, and professors of educational administration—that leadership requires a fundamental understanding and knowledge of teaching and learning.

A pedagogically centered leader not only knows about learning but also knows and understands the craft of teaching as a skilled professional. A pedagogically centered leader understands the complex interaction between teacher and child and hones this understanding by going through a high-quality educational leadership program.

It is our hope that the conversation begun in 1947 through NCPEA continues and advances the profession of leadership preparation in education into the mid-twenty-first century and beyond.

Introduction

This is a report from a special task force of the National Council of Professors of Educational Administration. It is a report to the membership and to the profession at large, written by five scholar-practitioners of NCPEA who have spent a good part of their careers preparing practitioners and scholars for the field of educational leadership. Nearly all have been principals and superintendents, and several have worked in the private sector as well (a complete description of all of the coauthors appears in the section titled "Meet the Coauthors and NCPEA").

The report is an attempt to piece together the trends and forces currently impacting preparation and practice and put them into focus around the theme of where we want to be as a professional field in 2050. The report is separated into three major sections, each comprising at least two chapters. The first section is "Conjectures," which are described as informed speculation consisting of *continuities* and *discontinuities*. In this section a major effort was made to avoid hindsight bias in constructing responses to the trends that surround our field today.

The next section is "Challenges." Here the task force examined the problems and issues facing educational leadership followed by a discussion of the need for *social justice* as the platform for determining the common good and purpose of schooling in a democratic society.

The final section is dedicated to "Promises," in which we present a portrait of a way of examining leadership that includes both the art and science of our work, some ideas regarding reframing preparation in contemporary settings, and a chapter sketching out what we envision as an approach to a more radical re-centering of our field. In this section we see a different vision. Instead of viewing teaching and learning as embedded in management, we propose to center management in matters of pedagogy, and a critical pedagogy at that.

This perspective is more than a notion of distributed leadership that still preserves traditional managerial hierarchies and the separation of teaching and leading in the schools as well as in the colleges and universities that prepare teachers and administrators. We believe that this bifurcation is no longer tenable given the internal and external pressures at work within and upon our field. We propose the concept of *pedagogically centered leadership* as a new dynamism. We see distinct conceptual and practical advantages to this shift.

It is our hope that this special report is a jump-start to a different kind of conversation about leading schools in the nation that moves beyond the simplistic business and accountability models now being imposed on the education enterprise and, if continued, will do enormous damage to the fabric of democratic schooling and the ethic of public service, which continue to animate our preparation programs and constitute the cornerstone of our practice.

Part I

Conjectures

Since 1945, however, leaders really have had the ability to change history. Khrushchev and Kennedy came close to doing so in 1962. Nuclear weapons leave us no margin for error, no second chance. Mistakes used to cause decline and fall; now they cause Nightfall. For the first time in history, leadership really is decisive. We can only hope that our age, like most before it, gets the thought it needs.

—Ian Morris (2010), *Why the West Rules—For Now* (p. 616)

Chapter One

At the Crossroads

We live and work in contested times. Our professional field is peopled with many individuals, groups, and agencies that make claims about its perceived defects and strengths. There are those who toil to improve the schools by working harder, those who want to change what the nature of the work is in leading the schools, and those who want to abolish the current leadership in the schools and institutions that have historically prepared them. The goal?—to re-place these and their traditions with business models.

While we disagree with some of our critics and their antidotes to improving school leadership, we wish to underscore that not only defenders but also critics firmly agree that *educational leadership is the critical ingredient without which K–12 public schools cannot be improved.*

In proffering its diagnosis and recommendations, the National Council of Professors of Educational Administration (NCPEA) Task Force determined that it would stake out a different course for examining and formulating changes for the schools and school leadership, as well as how leaders of the future should be pre-pared—to conceptually stretch and thereby force ourselves to think beyond the status quo.

As authors who are educational leaders, we rejected the taken-for-granted starting point of rolling the present into the future. This would be an example of "hindsight bias." Instead, we endeavored to take the future and roll it back to the present, with the result of proffering interpretations of our field in a new and different way.

We saw several advantages to this reversal. First, it avoided the inevitable problem of cementing current school operations as the epitome of institutional development. We wanted to unfreeze the field, allowing it to be seen as a developmental continuum where we could map the evolution of practices and beliefs from a different angle on a larger course.

Second, this approach to positioning current practices would enable us to both conceptually and intellectually reconstruct the relational bridge between schools and society. We recognized almost immediately that the advantage of this connection would take us to the nexus for any true consideration of improving social justice in both schools and society.

We believe that this challenge could not come at a more opportune time. The United States' demographic profile has undergone a profound transformation. US Census data show that the Hispanic population has grown 43 percent from 2000 and that one in four is Latino, specifically youth under the age of eighteen. The current majority white population is expected to decline to only 50.8 percent in 2040 and become a minority population by 2050, when it will only comprise 46.3 percent (Reddy, 2011, p. A2).

Clearly, the changing face of the United States, wherein the majority will become the minority, represents a prescient symbolic moment and one in which we think about other likely changes.

UNPACKING THE PRESENT-FUTURE DILEMMA

Humans make sense of the future by reflecting on the past. Some writers assert that we manage the unknown by placing various stimuli "into some kind of framework" (Starbuck & Milliken, 1998, p. 51). At the intersection of these two time constructs (past = future) is a process of sense making or thinking that, as Weick (1995) speculates, "uses retrospective accounts to explain surprises" (p. 4).

"Surprises" are one of the inevitable challenges, even hazards, of trying to grasp the future and creating a coherent agenda of potential change actions to account for it. Weick says that "to understand sense making is also to understand how people cope with interruptions" (p. 5). Postmodernists, for whom the status quo should be disrupted, would likely see these "surprises" or "interruptions" as *discontinuities*.

The NCPEA task force used two kinds of data sources in constructing a 2050 conjectural platform from which to work from the imagined future back to the present. These are shown in figure 1.1.

The first data set comprised existing trends that are discernible at the present. These are the *continuities*. However, the "surprises" or "interruptions" shown on hypothetical trend lines B, C, and E represent the *discontinuities*. The one on trend line E, for example, could be the financial meltdown caused by mortgage bubble bursting that plummeted the American economy into a profound recession and reverberated across worldwide financial markets.

That "surprise" pushed some nations' economic systems into potential collapse without a financial bailout (Fox, 2009). Other global "interruptions" include unpredictable catastrophes of modern times, such as New Orleans's Hurricane Katrina, the Japanese earthquake and tsunami, and the Arab uprisings leading to a domino collapse of dictatorships in the Middle East.

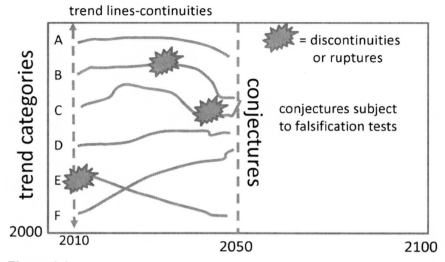

Figure 1.1.

We call the year 2050 a platform. However, this metaphor con-
notes a stability that we believe is not credible. It is rather a cluster
of conjectures. A conjecture is a guess built on "evidence insufficient for definite knowledge" (*Webster's Seventh New Collegiate
Dictionary*, 1971, p. 176). A conjecture is a way of framing selected stimuli or phenomena looking backward into the future in a
way that aligns the discontinuities of the present into some sort of
meaningful pattern.

As a conjecture, this pattern should be one that is subject to
testing for verification—that is, its truthfulness. This approach to
discerning the truth was philosopher Karl Popper's (1965) doctrine
of falsifiability in the scientific testing of conjectures.

Popper (1902–1994) rejected authority or even public polling as
a strategy for discerning whether a conjecture or a narrative could
be considered truthful. Even observation and perception contained
sources of error. We find compelling his notion that the only way a

conjecture can be potentially considered true is that every attempt
has been made to show its falseness—only then could it be considered tentatively true.

In creating this document, we built on Popper's notions of conjecture and refutation by adding the idea that no individual conjecture or hypothesis can be tested in isolation because all rest on
clusters of assumptions. The solution to this dilemma was to subject those assumptions *en bloc* (Butts, 1999). We proposed that our
total assertions for this work be tested *en bloc*.

The principal way any conjecture can be tested is to stipulate the
grounds on which it could be declared false. This was how Popper
(1965) differentiated between science and nonscience (see pp.
228–30 in the original source). According to Popper, any proponent
who stakes out a claim that his or her facts or arguments should be
accepted as true but who does not submit to a test of falsification
forfeits any claim of being considered truthful. In so doing, Popper
declared Marxism unscientific, and we would suggest that the
ideology of neoliberalism falls into a similar trap.

In creating our cluster of conjectures from both trends representing *continuities* and in taking into account those "surprises" or
"interruptions" as *discontinuities* of which we are currently aware,
we subjected them to stipulations as to how, if they are to be taken
seriously, they could also be falsified. First, we must indicate that
we view neither the continuities nor the discontinuities as *progress*.

WHATEVER COMES TO PASS IS NOT NECESSARILY PROGRESS

Current times are marked by proponents as an age in which whatever they want to come to pass becomes, in the eyes of those
viewing it, *inevitable*. We tried hard to avoid this trap because
progress is an idea and not a fact. The idea that things become

better over time has been shown by Nisbet (1980) to be a teleology—that is, true by definition (p. 21) because "it cannot be empiri-
cally or logically verified" (p. 6).

We see few socioeconomic-political trends as *inevitable*. We do
see them as "constructed by whom or what?" We recognize that
some are very powerful and exceptionally well financed. We see
very few as representing *progress*.

CONJECTURES AS CONTINUITIES FROM CURRENT PATTERNS

Here are some of the conjectures that are currently emergent. They
are derived from international trends discernible today. Why an
international starting point? Critical theorist Michael Apple (2011)
provides an excellent rationale, which takes as its starting point the
notion that

> nearly all educational policies and practices are strongly influ-
> enced by an increasingly integrated international economy that
> is subject to severe crises; that reforms and crises in one country
> have significant effects in others; and that immigration and pop-
> ulation flows from one nation or area to another have tremen-
> dous impacts on what counts as official knowledge, what counts
> as a responsive and effective education, what counts as appro-
> priate teaching . . . all of these social and ideological dynamics
> and many more are now fundamentally restructuring what edu-
> cation does, how it is controlled, and who benefits from it
> throughout the world. (pp. 222–23)

In the past, the creation of standards for educational leaders has
been centered in the United States. However, it is clear that educational leadership must be connected to international issues because,

as Nancy Fraser (2007) clearly points out, the causes of much so-cial injustice (defined as "participatory parity," p. 21) in the world today

> include the financial markets, "offshore factories," investment regimes, and governance structures of the global economy, which determine who works for a wage and who does not; the information networks of global media and cyber technology, which determine who is included in the circuits of communica-tive power and who is not; and the bio-politics of climate, dis-ease, drugs, weapons, and biotechnology, which determine who will live long and who will die young. (p. 25)

Social injustices in the United States are now connected to social injustices in the world in a way hardly imagined just twenty years ago. In fact, Fraser argues that if we confine confronting social justice issues solely to the "state-territorial principle," we will per-petuate them because they are not confined to such states. She advocates the "all-affected principle," which is that "all those af-fected by a given social structure or institution have moral standing as subjects of justice in relation to it" (p. 25).

We took heed of Apple's perspective that "we need to think internationally, not only to see the world from below, but to see the social world *relationally*. In essence, this requires that we under-stand that in order for there to be a 'below' in one nation, this usually requires that there be an 'above' both in that nation and in those nations with which it is connected in the global political economy" (2011, p. 225).

It is because US educational leadership is linked to the leader-ship challenges globally that educational leaders and the professors who prepare them must be cognizant of the emerging international challenges facing all nations. Global warming, the increasingly interconnected financial markets, and the threat of terrorism impact most nations on the planet; likewise, social injustices cannot be confined or resolved only within a single nation-state. It is because of this compounded condition that we present some of the most pressing issues facing the world through mid-century.

To provide the broadest canvas upon which to envision the role of schools in the fabric of the state, one must come to grips with the broad brush of history. As we paint the kinds of trends that could be called *continuities*, we underscore Russett's (2010) observation that "human affairs do not progress in a nice linear advance, but rather by ups and downs" (p. 16).

The following list of trends is not exhaustive because that is not the purpose of our publication. Rather, the purpose is to indicate that when forecasting mid-century developments, one must be concerned with consistent patterns but also be prepared for the ruptures of unexpected breaks in them.

Globalization

Globalization "is the process by which markets integrate world-wide" (Spence, 2011, p. 28). It seems very likely that globalization will continue as a dominant force, worldwide, with its emphasis on market-driven economies, neoliberal political agendas, and the use of collective security arrangements ("Global Progress Report, 2010," 2010, p. 3).

Morris (2010) reports that some individuals on America's National Intelligence Council see China's economic output catching up to the United States in 2036. Other thoughtful agencies see this event occurring nearer 2025, and some expert economists as early as 2016 (p. 583).

One of the most important trends in globalization is the impact in the United States with widening socioeconomic gaps and a more entrenched classist society where "the result is growing disparities in income and employment . . . with highly educated workers enjoying more opportunities and workers with less education facing declining employment prospects and stagnant incomes" (Spence, 2011, p. 29). There is every reason to believe that this trend will continue.

Yet the solution, as it pertains to educational leadership, is not simple; Spence attests, "As important as education is, it cannot be the whole solution; the United States will not educate its way out of its problems" (p. 39). Part of the solution, according to Spence, is to reform the tax structure and create a flatter income distribution, "suggesting that tradeoffs between market forces and equity are possible" (p. 40).

The Decline in the Reality of a Major War

The continuing decline of the threat of war between major powers is another continuity. Russett's (2010) study of wars (from 1885 through 2001) found that three factors made a huge difference in whether nations went to war: democracy, trade, and nongovernmental organizations. When these factors interacted together, they became "mutually reinforcing" because they created "a system of feedback loops that increasingly fosters peace" (p. 15).

Despite Russett's analysis, Morris (2010) indicates that the East's war-making capacity may reach parity with the West at 2050 (p. 583). Despite this prediction, Glaser (2011) observes that "current international conditions should enable the United States and China to protect their vital interests without posing large threats to each other" (p. 83).

A Worldwide Freshwater Crisis amid Global Warming

It is estimated that by mid-century "the demand for water will increase by 50 percent with each additional generation" (Peterson & Posner, 2010, p. 31). At the present time, "an estimated 884 million people world-wide do not have access to clean drinking water, and 2.5 billion lack adequate sanitation" (p. 32). Climate change will accelerate existing demands on the world's freshwater supply. Some estimate that by 2021, Lake Mead, which supplies water to Los Angeles, San Diego, and Las Vegas, will run dry.

At the same time, global warming is occurring, which could add fifty feet to the current sea levels. The North Pole will be ice-free by 2040 (Morris, 2010, p. 599). Climate change is nonlinear, and its interconnectedness with everything else is so complex as to defy prediction at this point.

The Crucial Bilateral Relationship: China and the United States

China has emerged as a world power: "China's economy doubles in size every half-dozen years and will probably be the worlds' largest before 2030" (Morris, 2010, p. 12). The *Economist* ("For-Profit Colleges," 2010) flatly declared, "It is probably the most important relationship of today's world, and even more of tomorrow's," and warned, "If the United States and China cannot co-operate, what hope of stemming climate change and the spread of nuclear weapons, or returning the global economy to a path of stable growth?" (p. 25).

China holds about $800 billion in assets in order to enable Americans to buy Chinese goods (Morris, p. 585). Such mutuality suggests, at least at this point, high interdependence between the two nations. The reality is that the United States is China's largest trading partner (Jisi, 2011, p. 72).

Christensen (2011) points out that it is in the interests of both the United States and China that China become more assertive regionally and globally by keeping a check on North Korea and Iran, and that "Washington should portray the prospect of cooperation not as a request based on U.S. national interests, but as a means through which Beijing can pursue its own interests" (p. 66). Other futurists also see Brazil as a new global power (Sweig, 2010).

The Technological Transformation of the World

Some technology pundits predict that by 2045 it will be possible to upload human minds into machines (Morris, 2010, p. 593). If one examines the trend lines and the pace of technology, the prediction is more than plausible, since every eighteen months since 1965, the ability of computer calculating capacity and memory has doubled.

One national defense agency in the United States has been developing a brain interface project that could construct computers from enzymes and DNA molecules to implant in the heads of soldiers so that they could communicate without radios. The National Science Foundation has indicated that "network-enabled telepathy" may be realized in the 2020s (Morris, p. 595). The implications of these developments for education would be profound and approaching "the greatest discontinuity in history" at the intersection of "genetics, robotics, nanotechnology, and computing" (Morris, p. 592). Such innovations seem as far-fetched to us today as cell phones, the Internet, and Facebook would have been to our grandparents.

Continued Threats of Global Terrorism

Farrall's (2011) review of al Qaeda boldly states that

> since fleeing Afghanistan to Pakistan's tribal areas in late 2001, al Qaeda has founded a regional branch in the Arabian Peninsula and acquired franchises in Iraq and the Maghreb. Today, it has more members, greater geographic research, and a level of ideological sophistication and influence it lacked ten years ago. (p. 128)

In addition to the United States, terrorist attacks have occurred in Spain, England, Kenya, Tanzania, Indonesia, India, Jordan, Iraq, Somali, and Chechnya, and one was foiled in Australia in 2009 (Farrall, 2011). As Schultz and Dew (2006) have recognized, "These strikes are now recognized as part of a global Salafi jihad movement, which combines a radical and puritanical interpretation of Islam with the use of deadly terrorist operations" (p. 260). The continued presence of lethal attacks is likely to continue for many years.

RUPTURES OR DISCONTINUITIES

Ruptures in trends are surprises few anticipated. Betts (2010) commented on Nassim Taleb's observation that "most world-changing developments turn out to be predicted by no one, the result of highly improbable events outside of analysts' equations" (p. 193). Such unpredictable events provide the discontinuities of our times.

Worldwide Financial Meltdown

Perhaps the most important rupture on the current state of affairs worldwide was the financial meltdown that turned into the "great recession" of the early twenty-first century. Built on the fallacy of the rational market hypotheses (Fox, 2009), this approach assumed that government regulation was unnecessary and that the market itself contained enough balances and counterbalances, as well as all the required information, to right and regulate itself (Cassidy, 2009, p. 97).

Unfortunately, within the dominant economic model there was "no place for stupidity, ignorance, or herd behavior" (Cassidy, p. 102). The ensuing monetary catastrophe in the mortgage industry in the United States "will be remembered as the great scam of the early twenty-first century" (Stiglitz, 2010, p. 77).

A consequence of the American-generated financial meltdown is that "the American version of capitalism is, if not in full disrepute, then at least no longer dominant" (Birdsall & Fukuyama, 2011, p. 46). Another was that the G-7 was replaced by the G-20. They went on to add:

In the next decade, emerging-market and low-income countries are likely to modify their approach to economic policy further, trading the flexibility and efficiency associated with the free-market model for domestic policies meant to ensure greater resilience in the face of competitive pressures and global economic trauma. They will become less focused on the free flow of capital, more concerned with minimizing social disruption through social safety net programs, and more active in supporting domestic industries. (Birdsall & Fukuyama, 2011, p. 46)

Technology Surprises—The Arab Spring

Information access has escalated in leaps and bounds for many parts of the world. Schmidt and Cohen (2010) predict, "The advent and power of connection technologies—tools that connect people to vast amounts of information and to one another—will make the twenty-first century all about surprises" (p. 75).

More than half of the world's population (seven billion people) has access to either cell phones or the Internet. Each individual in the world can become connected and "any person, regardless of living standard or nationality, is given a voice and the power to effect change" (Schmidt & Cohen, p. 75). In 2000 Pakistan had approximately three hundred thousand cell phone users, which by 2010 had grown to one hundred million.

The use of this technology has spawned a new type of protest. Messages on Facebook and Twitter created international incidents in Moldova in 2009 following street protests that brought the downfall of the government and led to the first non-Communist government in the past fifty years (Schmidt & Cohen, 2010). Additionally, the death of an Egyptian blogger, Khaled Said, by the police triggered the uprising in that country (Anderson, 2011).

While technology per se was not the cause of the Arab Spring, which brought sea changes in Tunisia, Egypt, and Libya in 2011, it was undeniably a component in it as activists shared ideas and tactics with one another (Anderson, 2011).

The Tea Party Rupture in Mainstream Politics

The rise of the Tea Party has been called "the most controversial and dramatic development in U.S. politics in many years" (Mead, 2011, p. 29). It began as a technological rant of a financial reporter on the floor of the Chicago Mercantile Exchange on CNBC in February 2009 (p. 29). Picked up by Fox News and backed by independent wealthy sponsors, it soon grew into a full-fledged political protest movement.

Mead has analyzed the Tea Party manifestation and likens it to an expression of populist sentiment with deep roots in American history, beginning with the election of Andrew Jackson as president by what became known as "Jacksonian democracy."

Mead also observes, "Antiestablishment populism has been responsible for some of the brightest, as well as some of the darkest, moments in U.S. history" (p. 33). It is based on the "commonsense tradition of the Scottish Enlightenment. This philosophy—that moral, scientific, political, and religious truths can be ascertained by the average person—is more than an intellectual conviction in the United States; it is a cultural force" (Mead, p. 34).

The Tea Party may not survive in the twenty-first century, but if it should not, "other voices of populist protest will take its place" (Mead, p. 44). To a certain extent, the rationale for the dabbling in American education by billionaires Bill Gates, Eli Broad, Michael Dell, and John Walton are denials that any special educational expertise is required to know how to "fix" American education ("Grading the Moneymen," 2011).

THE EDUCATIONAL LEADERSHIP FIELD: DYNAMICS OF CONSOLIDATION AND STANDARDIZATION

Intellectually and politically, the field of educational administration has been in a period of consolidation and standardization for the past twenty years. It is still a strong trend in the field. Collins (1998) has called this kind of conceptual/intellectual retrenchment *scholasticism*. He defines it as the "worshipping [of] exalted texts from the past which are regarded as containing the completion of all wisdom. Eminence here goes to those persons who make themselves the most impressive guardians of the classics" (p. 31).

In the field of educational administration, such worshipping of the classics of the past is part of the creation of the ISLLC-ELCC standards. These standards are ostensibly based on research without an acknowledgment that (a) research rarely creates definitive answers to complex problems and is inevitably embedded in specific contexts extremely difficult to extract, abstract, and transfer; and (b) whatever the research has been, it has not been able to resolve such complex matters as the achievement gap (English, 2003).

Basing standards of practice on skill sets derived from such research bears heeding a warning from Pierre Bourdieu:

> If the way science is conducted in the educational research field produces findings which yield disappointing results when applied to practice, it may be that it is because its science is being impeded by influences with preset agendas of *what* the outcomes should be and *how* they should be; namely, in line with the already decided political discourse and its legitimated values and consecrated knowledge systems. (Grenfell, 2007, p. 249)

Significantly, there have been no new breakthroughs in understanding the nature of leadership because *scholasticism* as a movement requires a political consensus. The reason is that there are no empirical means to demonstrate leadership because a sociocultural construction has been "captured" by the formation of a "knowledge base." The dilemma is that "there are no a priori meta-criteria to separate science from non-science in educational administration" (English, 2002, p. 109).

Attempts by such agencies as the National Research Council's (NRC) (2002) *Scientific Research in Education* to only recognize studies employing "true" science are only possible when inquiry is aimed at *verification*. On the other hand, actual *scientific discovery* "is irrational, unpredictable, and rule independent" (English, 2007, p. 3). A paramount concern with methods (in this case, quantitative methods advanced by NRC) was criticized by Bourdieu when he observed that "it is not the technical sophistication of methodological tools . . . but their mindless refinement to fill the vacuum created by the absence of theoretical vision" (Wacquant, 1992, p. 28).

Unintended Consequences Become Apparent

Paradoxically, raising expectations for improved performance can result in lowered standards. There have been several unintended consequences of this long process of *scholasticism* in educational administration. Perhaps the most paradoxical is that, although launched in order to raise the bar in the preparation of educational administrators, it has actually worked to lower expectations.

The standards themselves were never designed to examine all of the functions of leadership—only that which was identified as the "core technology" related to selected aspects of instruction in schools. When used to examine the efficacy of a preparation program via state or national accreditation, they serve to reduce that program to only what is included in it. And they have prompted the transport of preparation away from the university environment as the intellectual/conceptual place where leadership alternatives may be examined to sites where current practice is reproduced and reified (English, 2006).

Thus, just as the neoliberal foundations and think tanks have worked to deprofessionalize leadership preparation for political reasons (Broad Foundation & Thomas B. Fordham Institute, 2003; Hess, 2004), the ISLLC-ELCC standards enable preparation to be relocated in the marketplace and to be pursued by "for-profit" marketers.

Shifting Power and Legitimacy in the Field of Preparation

Consider Bourdieu's idea that specific fields exist (education being one), constitute a separate social universe, and contain hierarchies of authority and power that are in constant flux. Agents and actors within fields and within our educational leadership field reach for domination by advancing claims that in effect increase their visibility and power. Bourdieu commented that differences with a field's structure account for the struggles for specific stakes within it. No matter how autonomous the field appears to be, the internal conflict is never completely free of external forces whose actions may contribute to the advancement or loss of power within a specific field. Thus the power relationships between the "conservatives" and the "innovators," the orthodox and the heretical, the old and the new, are greatly dependent on the state of external struggles and on the reinforcement that one or another may find from without (1993, pp. 184–85).

The idea of a field comprising competitive forces vying for legitimacy was described by Bourdieu and Passeron (2000), who said that such "competition is . . . necessary because legitimacy is indivisible: there is no agency to legitimate the legitimacy-giving agencies" (p. 18).

The current competition within the educational leadership field can be seen as a continuing struggle for legitimacy. No one is a neutral player in that all represent interests and perspectives linked to certain external constituencies. The real question we pose is this: Which agenda is better suited to be in the public's best interests? It is against this backdrop that we positioned this report.

Schools are neither culturally neutral places nor socially free-floating institutions educating the young. In most nations of the world, schools are institutions of the state, or at least regulated by the state. They are therefore embedded in the affairs of state, firmly located in the problems and policies of the state. Most nations of the world see the schools as places to perpetuate the rule of the state, and the United States is no exception.

In every society, the prevailing belief system has been largely created by those with the most power—typically, elderly males belonging to the majority ethnic and religious group, who also run the dominant institutions of the society. It is notable, for example, that "almost all religions rationalize a subordinate position for women and explain that inequalities of fortune are to be accepted as part of God's great (if mysterious) plan" (Barry, 2005, p. 27).

IMPLICATIONS FOR PROFESSIONAL PREPARATION

A review of the continuities and discontinuities of our times leaves an indelible impression of the disjunction between what schools do and what they don't do when they are placed into any reasonable or logical portrait on the canvas of the next fifty years. In similar fashion, this disjunction is also apparent in the preparation of leaders to work in those schools.

While nearly everyone agrees that leadership is what in medieval times was called "the philosopher's stone"—that is, the magic device for turning lead into gold (English, 2011a)—there is still no clear approach or path to providing such leaders, no matter how desperately needed. The following sections detail our observations regarding where we are now.

Preparation Occurs in Contested Social Space

The field of educational leadership preparation comprises a plethora of individuals and agencies vying for legitimacy and power. Bourdieu and Passeron (2000) indicate that such contestation will go on indefinitely because there is no supra-agency that bestows legitimacy and power. It has to be claimed and won from the other players in the field.

In fact, over the last fifty years the players in this social space have multiplied and vied for power and legitimacy. When shown as an interlocking *field*, a term by Bourdieu (1993) defined as "a separate social universe having its own laws of functioning independent of those of politics and economy" (p. 162), we see what Foucault (1972) called an *apparatus.* A glimpse of the current *apparatus* is shown in figure 1.2 (from English & Papa, 2010, p. 12).

If such a sketch had been drawn in 1947, when, for example, NCPEA was founded, some agencies would not be represented at all (such as NCATE, CCSSO, UCEA, AERA, and NPBEA). Over the years individuals and agencies have exerted claims to legitimacy, and thus to power and authority, through the normal activities of writing reports, seeking to expand membership, and banding with other actors and agencies to expand their sphere of influence.

In the words of Bourdieu (1993), "The state of power relations in this struggle depend on the overall degree of autonomy possessed by the field, that is, the extent to which it manages to impose its own norms and sanctions on the whole set of producers, including those who are closest to the dominant pole of the field of power and therefore most responsive to external demands" (p. 40). Bourdieu further indicates that the autonomy of the field varies from one time to another and one national tradition to another. We certainly see this with respect to the preparation of educational leaders.

He indicates that "in an ideal, fully autonomous *field*, only the *field* mechanisms themselves would determine their product, independently from any influence of other *fields*" (Grenfell, 2007, p.

247). He also avers that "what is at stake here is the extent to which a *field* can operate according to its own logic of practice" and adds, "A scientific *field* is objective to the extent to which it is autonomous" (Ibid.).

We believe that the true partners of the field of educational preparation are professors and practitioners. We also believe that the intrusion of other authorities and agencies in the preparation process have coalesced around ideas that compromise autonomy and impede the development of improved practice in the field. Federal and state agencies have been promoting standards of practice that have frozen both our outlook and preparation in the status quo and with it all of the educational and social inequalities that also exist. Today's "good practice" is not necessarily tomorrow's reform.

Standardization Is a Tactic to Claim Legitimacy and Enhance One's Power in the Field

Applying Bourdieu's thinking to the educational leadership field, we see the rise of a variety of agencies with the power to apply sanctions—that is, deny to institutions that prepare educational leaders the legitimacy to do so, which elevates and expands such agencies. The rise of powerful governmental agencies such as state departments of education and NCATE are testimony to the advancement to their claims of legitimacy in the field.

The tools of power in these two cases are (1) the initiation of testing (the ISLLA or surrogate) as a key to licensure and practice from state departments of education, and (2) the use of accreditation to deny legitimacy to institutions of preparation (NCATE) that are linked to state accreditation programs. A denial of accreditation that acts as a form of policing can result, at least for public agencies, in a short route to extinction.

The power of these two supra-agencies is able to be exercised as long as the field remains autonomous, managed by its own logic and laws. However, within the last decade the rise of neoliberal foundations and think tanks regarding the privatization and commodification of public spaces, and with it educational preparation, has been a political force working to reshape relationships and ideas regarding changes within the field.

Neoliberal think tanks such as Heritage Foundation, the American Enterprise Institute, and the Broad and Gates Foundations deny the efficacy of the structures of the field at all, and some posit that licensure and professional preparation standards and programs are unnecessary. This stance amounts to a denial of the entire field of educational leadership preparation and a negation of its legitimacy (English, 2011b).

As the authors of this publication, we see the continued pursuit of leadership standardization as a distinctively negative trend in our field for the following reasons:

- Leadership cannot be standardized.
- Management, rather than leadership, is more likely to be so structured.
- While problems facing leadership may be categorized, they cannot be standardized because they are almost always context dependent.
- Leadership is both an art and a science, and both have to be considered in the preparation process and in research perspectives about it (Heilbrunn, 1996).
- Business models of leadership with attendant metaphors of measurement, marketing, for-profit mind-sets, and accounting dehumanize schools and erode the fragile ethos of public service upon which a profession centered on the education of children has long depended.
- The agenda of the philanthrocapitalists is not about reforming anything. Rather, it is about refining the status quo.

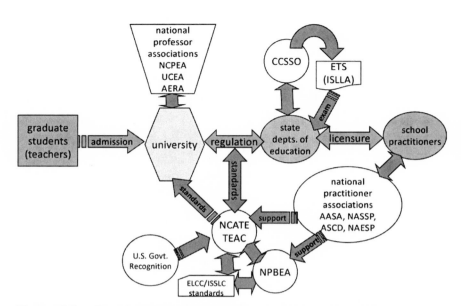

Figure 1.2.   Reprinted with permission from the publisher, Pro-Active Publications

It is our hope in writing this publication that we take heed of the way we think, speak, and act in preparing educational leaders and in researching good practices of leaders. We also hope that it serves as a *positive rupture* in the current trends with which we are contending and that by mid-century we have left this period in the first half of the new century.

As Henze and Arriaza (2006) note, "Any serious effort to reform schools to be more equitable and socially just . . . has to consider the role of language in constructing the social identities of those who make up the school community and the power relations among them. . . . Discourse not only mirrors their practice, it is their practice" (p. 164).

Chapter Two

The Digital Age and Learning to Lead in It

Josie, age seven, described her technology use as follows:

> What I can do with a computer is go on 2,000 different websites, go on Google, open files, go on Firefox for music or DVD mode. What I can do with an iPad is play games, download applications, go on Google, check the weather on the weather application, check the application for mail to see who has written me or my mommy. What I can do with an iPhone is play games, call and text people, take pictures and send them in a message, and of course, use Google, check mail, weather, etc. One of my favorite websites is PBSKids.org. (personal communication, February 17, 2011)

GROWING UP DIGITALLY

A defining characteristic of mid-century life is that children and youth will have grown up digitally (Tapsott, 2009). The new literacy will reflect "a complex [set] of intertwined cognitive skills" not understood by most adults of our generation (Brown, 2000, p. 13).

Based on his interview of three hundred youths under twenty years old, Tapsott coined the term "Net Generation" (i.e., digital learner) to describe the pervasive phenomenon of children and youth who are digitally comfortable, literate, and even innovative. Many play sophisticated online games, communicate using chat sites, and are proficient surfers of the Internet and users of Google, Facebook, Twitter, smartphones, and more—they are unlike many adults living today.

Many young people would rather text than talk, and they want to communicate and learn with technology that can fit in their hands and ears. Tech-savvy principals can, it is expected, successfully build capacity for their schools by leading with technology and developing teams that know how to enhance student learning, address cybersafety, and more (Grady, 2011).

The digital learning curve for many baby boomers is steep. In contrast, "Net Geners" will be entering schools acculturated differently, not just as learners but also as social beings (Brown, 2000). For example, mid-century leaders and youth may experience virtual emotions and events just as they would in the real world. Taken to an extreme, they will not distinguish reality-induced from virtually induced emotions, friendships, and experiences in the way we do today.

If a collapse should occur in the distinctions made today between the real world and virtual world, an entirely new lexicon will emerge that signifies that what is virtual *is* real. Put differently, there may be a blend, a type of seamlessness, between these worlds, with far less attention given to what is not "real"—because if something is felt or experienced, regardless of the medium, it will be real. Already people believe that they can show respect, caring, and genuine feelings electronically.

DRAMATIC SHIFTS IN LITERACY WILL RESHAPE LEADERSHIP

Dramatic shifts in literacy occurring today that will be "normative" in the future include the following:

- The use and interpretation of multimedia texts that heavily incorporate image and screen literacy
- A facility for multiprocessing using different technologies
- The use of multimedia genres in learning and teaching
- The ability to navigate vast amounts of information and function as a reference librarian
- Engagement in discovery-based learning that is action based and supported by cognitive apprenticeships (Brown, 2000)

Brown has built his own life-world of the future using these technological trends and cognitive psychological models of learning. In his mind, knowledge that is formal and tacit will emerge from the participation of leaders, teachers, and students in communities of practice for which intelligence, knowledge, and expertise will be valued as belonging not to the individual so much as to the community.

These dimensions of knowing will be "distributed across a broader matrix" within learning communities committed to the practice of "learning to learn" (p. 15). Socially constructed understandings will be nurtured in schooling environments for which praxis (theory that is enacted through practicing ideas) will drive theory and where theory will be "coerced" into a relationship with practice (Tapsott, 2009).

Digital learners will move into leadership and teaching roles having already lived their childhood, adolescence, and adulthood immersed in this kind of high-speed, interactive, global world. They will not be merely acclimated users of digital technology, like most adaptive adults today, but rather digital pedagogues whose intelligence will be different from ours—they will have greater leverage to "develop and superimpose [their] culture on the rest of society" (Tapsott, 2009, p. 2).

Net Geners will take over schools, just like every niche of society, bringing with them "their demographic muscle, media smarts, purchasing power, new models of collaborating and parenting, entrepreneurship, and political power" (Tapsott, p. 3).

As an activist collective, leaders of mid-century schools will be in a good position to alleviate the racial disintegration of schools and neighborhoods (discussed later). Because it is expected that they will be "more tolerant of diversity than their predecessors" (Tapsott, p. 6), these future leaders and teachers will likely not alienate people who, for example, declare themselves gay online. The long-standing phobias attached to our heteronormative societies will have faded.

Discrimination based on sexuality, class, gender, race, ethnicity, religion, and other differences will likely not be tolerated within these school communities. Instead of resorting to a "three strikes, you're out" mentality, school teams will foster understanding of difference for children and youth through education inside and outside their buildings. Open dialogue, cross-cultural group activity, and discovery of personal and cultural identities will be ongoing activities.

Mid-century leaders will teach their children from the time they are infants to understand, accept, and appreciate diversity. Many of these leaders of mid-century schools will care strongly about social justice and problems faced by society and will likely be concerned about the greater good, not just their careers or even campuses. Tapsott believes that the coming generation will be much more intensively engaged in civic activity within and across school communities. He says Net Geners prize and value freedom at all levels, including freedom of choice, customized options (e.g., curriculum, technology, products), and government for the people.

The Rejection of the Industrial-Age Teaching Model

In education, mid-century leaders will vigorously reject the Industrial-Age teaching model evident in hierarchical schools, opening up their schools and turning them into global communities. They may enact this transformation through civic engagement, mentoring programs for diverse learners, large-scale recruitment efforts, authentic learning and assessment, and more. They may work collectively on changing classrooms into vibrant, open communities by "forging a change in the model of pedagogy, from a teacher-focused approach based on instruction to a student-focused model based on collaboration" (Tapsott, 2009, p. 11).

No longer will teaching consist of one-way lectures and one-size-fits-all curriculum, except perhaps in the most isolated of schools and remote districts, where it may be difficult to attract quality teachers and teaching machines may be substituted for human teachers. Net Geners will be computer-literate teachers and leaders who will lead and learn as teams, whose thinking will be extended beyond stymied and regional mind-sets, whose growth will have been intertwined with the Internet, and whose discovery-based knowledge and curricula legitimate cyberspace learning (Grady, 2011).

Digital learners' evolving personal and global consciousness should benefit children within their locations and around the world. They will have the chance to respond to indigenous calls for worldwide justice. "The Invitation," a Native American poem (Mountain Dreamer, 2004), declares that how people act on behalf of children when they feel exhausted or incapable of taking action is a reflection of our core values and, hopefully, higher calling.

This poet also advises leaders and citizens to do what is needed for all children, regardless of where we live or how wealthy we are. She challenges us to "get up after the night of grief and despair, weary and bruised to the bone, and do what needs to be done for the children" (p. 17). She likewise wants to know if we "will stand in the center of the fire . . . [and] not shrink back."

To her, it is not vital where or what we have studied—what matters is our human core, or that which sustains us "from the inside when all else falls away" (p. 17). Indigenous perspectives on humanity and personhood may have value for mid-century civic leaders who can mobilize such inspirational messages.

What will mid-century leadership be like in the digital age for leaders for whom the learning and success of youth from all backgrounds will be a global concern? Will the passionate cry of storytellers, healers, and other "partial [or unofficial] leaders" (English, 2008) indigenous to our school communities influence the course of history as it unfolds? We must be prepared to lead our mid-century schools as part of the *Learning in Technology* era (Barnett & Archambault, 2010; Schrader, 2008).

How might schools of education, school districts, and community agencies prepare for the challenges associated with a cultural-technological revolution that could promote learning and fairness (e.g., equity, excellence, success) for all students and schools as well as disrupt fairness? Will complete leaders be ready to "stand in the center of the fire" (Mountain Dreamer, 2004, p. 17) to lead from the inside out, uniting forces to kindle the positive effects of change?

A Different Mind-set

The mid-century school leader will likely not have the leader's mind-set of today, which is stoic about monitoring and circumventing interruptions of this kind through work-arounds, policies, and other means. The Net Generation leader's world and priorities will be different—the online social media platform will be a merged socializing vehicle for many schools, for youth as well as adults (Peck, Mullen, Lashley, & Eldridge, 2011).

The unwanted advertising glut, perpetuated through Internet companies, that overwhelms and distracts us from the core purposes of teaching and learning is such that one cannot really fathom the complexity of this challenge. However, the mid-century leader will have a more finely attuned "antenna" for understanding what potentially distracts from and enhances the core mission of schools.

Leaders will probably have customizing control over and input into the design elements and other features of social networking software and other technologies. At a minimum, they will build knowledge assets over time with online problem-solving teams (Brown, 2000; Carnes, 2011).

School leaders will be immersed in pedagogical sense making of multimedia technology in learning and schoolwide delivery systems expected in higher-income schools. Paradoxically, such "technology enablers" as online learning and Internet access to learning tools for K–12 schools should significantly reduce racial and ethnic disparities as services and products that are accessible to a few become widely available.

Considering online learning within American universities, for example, trends suggest that by 2014, about 50 percent of students will be taking at least one course online (Christensen, Horn, Caldera, & Soares, 2011). Businesses have already cornered the market on a large sector of society and transforming exclusive universities and schools, with the for-profit goal of closing the gap between the "have" and "have-not" cultures (see Anderson & Herr, 2011).

TECHNOLOGICAL PROGRESS AS A CONTINUUM

If we envision the future as a continuum, at one extreme there might be schools that include "organizational cultural barriers that may limit the willingness or understanding of teachers to fully integrate technology in curriculum and instruction" (Lackney, 2011, p. 368). At the other would be fewer schools, perhaps a smaller num-

ber than expected, that are "well funded, motivated, and technologically literate enough to be well on their way to creating online
learning communities, and even virtual schools that offer distance
learning via web-based delivery" (p. 368).

Based on demographic trends, Lackney's projection that most
schools will be somewhere in the middle forecasts greater cultural
disparity than exists today. American schools have been resegregat-
ing for two decades and, given historical changes and legislative
decisions, will continue in this direction (Orfield & Lee, 2007).

Current schooling trends suggest that mid-century leaders will
be grappling with human rights, and the educational attainment of
all student groups will be that much harder and that much more
necessary. In the United States, it is expected that unfathomable
gaps in educational and economic success will occur among white
and nonwhite groups, partly owing to the reduced local control of
schools and districts over racial integration:

> The country's rapidly growing population of Latino and black
> students is more segregated than they have been since the 1960s
> and we are going backward faster in the areas where integration
> was most far-reaching. Under the new decision, local and state
> educators have far less freedom to foster integration than they
> have had for the last four decades. (Orfield & Lee, p. 4)

The widening socioeconomic gulf that is predicted means that, at
best, the positive effects of learning technologies and the distribution of them across US schools will be uneven and socially stratified (i.e., class based). Researchers (e.g., Davis, Davis, &
Williams, 2010) also foresee a pronounced variation in the access
and use of technology across schools in this nation, contrary to the
softened (and thus misleading) impression of cultural disparity that
Lackney says influential national surveys convey.

Learning through technology will be much more standard for
schools not burdened by socioeconomic hardship, insufficient
funding, and technology illiteracy (Lackney, 2011; Sterne, 2003).

In better-staffed and more elite learning-centered digital environments, principals will likely be invaluable in supporting teachers, and teachers in supporting students, for using hardware and software in ways both intended and unintended to promote the meaningful and relevant multimedia learning of all or most subject content (Creighton, 2011).

Learning technologies will be perpetuated by innovations in science, business, and economics, in particular, which will in turn serve these disciplines. "Technology-enabled instruction" that supports such "innovative learning strategies" as "self-directed learning and project-based learning" will be integral to the work of classroom teachers and principals (Lackney, p. 369; see also Peck et al., 2011).

THE SOCIAL CONTEXT OF TECHNOLOGY

The social context of technology in which new leaders will lead is simultaneously fluid and situated. Bourdieu (1985) describes *habitus* as subjectively embodied social knowledge or, more plainly, "second nature." English (2011a) related this sociological theory to the educational leadership field, envisioning it as a kind of theater of the mind in which power is a site of (uneven) distribution and struggle among the populace.

Creative leaders unmake and remake their social world, understanding dynamics of symbolic power, politics, and history in the constitution of social collectives. The leader cannot "see" the future and impose this vision detached from embodied histories and contextual realities; the mid-century leader will inhabit a "social world," using Bourdieu's logic, that "can be perceived and uttered in different ways" within "relatively indeterminate" social spaces (1985, p. 728) where possibility and the unknown are givens.

Leaders seize the opportunity to elicit and transform their world by inviting and producing plural perspectives that introduce an "element of play, of uncertainty" in their decision-making. Bourdieu (1985) refers to this mindscape as a "cognitive 'filling-in' [of] strategies that produce the meaning . . . of the social world by going beyond the directly visible attributes by reference to the future or the past" (p. 728).

The 2050 leader will not see schools as static, one-dimensional systems but rather as multidimensional social spaces where "occupants" of "dominant positions" "constantly [engage] in struggles of different forms" (Bourdieu, 1985, p. 736). A lesson here is that the social identity of any individual school will be important to its changing milieu. Furthermore, while schools will be products of history, visionary leaders must respect the embodied nature of the school's living history while enabling it to be changed by history.

TECHNOLOGY LEADERSHIP WITH POLICY AND PRACTICE

Visionary 2050 leaders will prepare for the responsibility of policy-making with regard to development, interpretation, and implementation. They will make "critical policy decisions regarding technology that will have repercussions on all aspects of education including school design" (Lackney, 2011, p. 372; see also Creighton, 2011). And 2050 leaders will be expected to do the following:

1. Model the use of new technologies, such as blogs, in communicating with students, parents, teachers, and the public.
2. Ensure that technology becomes integral to teaching twenty-first-century skills from critical thinking and problem solving to collaboration and information literacy in the classroom.
3. Boost Web applications and tools as key components of student learning.

4. Offer professional development in these technologies and deploy the online tools that help teachers create peer-led learning communities.

5. Require well-balanced assessments of student work, including project-based learning enhanced by technology tools, and better use of data from standardized testing assessments to help students improve their performances (as cited in Schachter, 2010, p. 42).

Likely incumbent upon leaders will be the task of finding resourceful ways for fostering student development and achievement using the learning community model for which large buildings and underfunded buildings will be more vigorously reshaped into smaller learning communities. As learning becomes much more virtual and web based, it must still take place in a physical space that fosters communication, interaction, and learning.

In this new environment, superintendents, school leaders, and others will become chief technology officers. This will be particularly necessary for smaller school districts with shrinking budgets, requiring the leadership function of chief technology officer. Thus, leaders will not be able to relegate to instructional support staff the role of technology leader. They will learn alongside other technology leaders, and when resources are sufficient, they will consult with technology integration specialists—quite likely at remote sites and even in other countries where technology jobs have been outsourced at cheaper rates.

The social space of learning through technology will change building arrangements. "Green" learning spaces and schools are being designed as the home base from which communities, libraries, and homes function. School buildings may become "home bases" of learning, not the institutions where all learning happens. Based on this trend, buildings will get smaller and greener, and schedules will change to accommodate more people engaged in off-campus learning activities.

Also, within high-performance schools, more teachers and students will participate in project-based, real-world learning (also known as experiential, service, and civic learning) directly in their own and more distant communities (Lackney, 2011; Papa, 2011a; Peck et al., 2011). More and more learning at school is already occurring nontraditionally (outside of classrooms and buildings), as can currently be observed by youngsters who use laptops and other technologies in study areas and on school grounds.

Technologically savvy 2050 educational leaders will allow the network-based concepts of flow, collaboration, and dynamism to help them rearrange classrooms not otherwise conducive to authentic twenty-first-century learning. Technology may become the new norm for differentiating instruction in ways that make learning engagement compatible with individual and cultural learning styles.

Part II

Challenges

If it is accepted that truly democratic education is education which sets itself the unconditional goal of enabling the greatest possible number of individuals to appropriate, in the shortest possible time, as completely and as perfectly as possible, the greatest possible number of the abilities which constitute school culture at a given moment, then it is clear that it is opposed both to traditional education, which aims to train and select a well-born elite, and to technocratic education, aimed at mass production of made-to-measure specialists.

—Pierre Bourdieu and Jean-Claude Passeron (1979), *The Inheritors* (pp. 75–76)

Chapter Three

Warning Signs of the Times

One useful approach to strategic thinking and planning indicates that as one identifies important negative or positive trends, participants should (1) control the controllable; (2) preempt the undesirable; and (3) prepare for the inevitable (Kaufman, Herman, & Watters, 1996).

As we look at the current scene in education, we see warning signs that if certain trends are continued, enormous damage could result to the schools and to the democratic society they serve. Our concerns are not only for what is occurring but also for what is not occurring. We identify each trend followed by one to three indicators (1 = we must control the forces that account for this trend; 2 = we must work to be sure this trend is not continued by opposing it; 3 = there is nothing we can do and so we should prepare for its continuance).

THE RESEGREGATION AND MARKETIZATION OF THE NATION'S PUBLIC SCHOOLS (1, 2)

The advancement of charter schools and voucher programs is accelerating the resegregation of the nation's school systems (Miron, 2010). Charter schools in some states are not required to educate special-needs students or accept students with limited English-speaking abilities. While the wealthy have always used schools to their advantage in order to promote their class-based interests (Bowles, Gintis, & Groves, 2005; Brantlinger, 2003; Bourdieu & Passeron, 1979), the enactment of charter legislation has increased the sorting of the haves and have-nots in American society.

Legislation that promotes charters and vouchers passes off the responsibility of poor schools to poor choices on the part of parents. It thus relieves the state of any responsibility for improving schooling for the poor via increased revenue support. It also opens the schools to marketization and increased "for-profit" vendors.

For example, in New York City, Joel Klein resigned after having served as the controversial chancellor of that system and forcing forms of privatization into the schools in the form of charters. After resigning as chancellor after eight years, Mr. Klein, a non-educator, went to work for Rupert Murdoch's News Corporation, which includes ownership of the *Wall Street Journal* and Fox TV (Klein, 2011).

Additionally, News Corporation owns Wireless Generation, an educational technology company that recently won a $1.5 million no-bid contract for installing a data system in the New York City schools and a similar $27 million no-bid contract to develop "assessment tracking software for the New York State Education Department," about which an official with Common Cause New York remarked, "It looks like a sweetheart deal that was cut, and no one was looking out for the taxpayer or the student" (Quillen, 2011, p.

18). It is estimated that the total market News Corporation is attempting to penetrate is valued at $500 billion per year (Adams & Vascellaro, 2010).

The advancement of charters and other "alternatives" to the traditional public schools also means opening what has been considered a "public service" mind-set, an orientation to serving students, to using monetary alternatives to support for-profit schemes to gain more "customers." Kimber and Ehrich (2011) have called this trend the "democratic deficit" because the proponents of marketing restructuring of the public-sector management are oblivious to the political nature of public management and "ignore that public servants are often motivated by factors other than higher pay. Indeed, public servants often cite public duty as a key motivating factor in their work" (p. 182). The result is what Rhodes (1994) has called "the hollow state," which is described as "the removal of public goods and services from the public sector and the reduction of citizens to customers or clients" (p. 180).

Turning schools over to educational management firms has become big business and is likely to increase in size in the future (Anderson & Herr, 2011).

THE DEMONIZATION OF TEACHER UNIONS (1, 2)

Neoliberal politicians, mostly (but not exclusively) Republicans, backed by lavishly funded right-wing think tanks and neoliberal philanthrocapitalists, have succeeded in giving teacher unions and school boards black eyes in the larger body politic. Teacher unions have become the favorite punching bag for standing as "obstacles" to what the neoliberals label "reforms" but which are really their political ideologies and agendas for exerting corporate-style management and marketization being implemented in the public schools (see Anderson & Pini, 2011; Riley, 2011).

The standard line for the so-called reformers of urban school systems when they bump into union resistance to their changes is to accuse them of putting the interests of adults before children (Klein, 2010; Rhee & Fenty, 2010), while their ideas regarding accountability, merit pay, and antitenure proposals, among others, are "right" and represent "only the interests of schoolchildren" (Rhee & Fenty, p. C2).

The blindness and naïveté of those calling themselves "reformers" (Klein, 2011) in saying that their antidotes are anything other than their own ideologies advanced as a moral crusade is a classic example of *misrecognition* of their own interests (Rhee, 2011). The "reforms" they advance are not neutral, and enhance these individuals' own power and control within a contested social field (see Bourdieu, 1999).

The real battle with teacher unions is about who controls teachers' work. Teachers lack the independence that historically belongs to other professions such as medicine and law (Lortie, 1969). Gunter (2002) points out that because teachers as a group lack the capability to determine for themselves entrance to the field and salary, and the political strength to act independently, they exercise the autonomy they do have through union membership. Thus, union collectivity offers a buffer between those who would seek to control teacher work activity and the protection offered to teachers to resist that intrusion and control.

Teacher unions do not usually tell teachers how to teach, so membership does not bring peer supervision into a reality. Rather, unions act to block management or other external forces from interfering in the classroom and undermining organizational freedom and choice. Installing merit pay schemes, denying teachers tenure, increasing standardized testing, and linking test performance to evaluation are all measures to extend control over teachers' work and make them more dependent on managerial whim and direction. The instrument through which they express that resistance to their loss of autonomy is the teacher union.

Unions would not exist if teachers did not feel they were fulfilling a necessary function. Seen from this perspective, what is perceived as an "obstacle" to some is seen by others as the key to professional independence and individual judgment as it pertains to one's sphere of work. While some "reformers" of the schools deny that "there is no war on teachers," they have no hesitation in saying simultaneously that there is "a war on the blunt and detrimental policies of teacher unions" (Hanushek, 2010, p. A17). It's more than getting rid of bad teachers, because it is also difficult to get rid of bad doctors, bad lawyers, or bad accountants. The real battle is about control of the work that goes on in schools.

THE DE-PROFESSIONALIZATION OF EDUCATIONAL LEADERSHIP PREPARATION (1, 2)

Schools of education, and educational leadership programs in particular, have come under fire by neoliberal politicians from both sides of the aisle, funded and pushed by right-wing think-tank pundits (Hess, 2003) and venture philanthrocapitalists such as Eli Broad (Riley, 2009).

The attacks accuse educational leadership programs of (a) not being selective enough; (b) not teaching hard management skills, which would be better acquired in business schools, law schools, or the military; and (c) constituting a "faulty pipeline" that limits educational leadership and creates a "harmful monopoly" because it limits talented people from coming into educational administration (Hess, 2003; Thomas B. Fordham Institute & Broad Foundation, 2003).

What lies behind this approach is what Bourdieu and Passeron (1979) have called "the ideology of charisma" and what Khurana (2002) of the Harvard Business School refers to as "the irrational quest for charismatic CEO's." The "ideology of charisma" is a way one uses to explain inequality of persons—in this case, leaders. As Bourdieu and Passeron explain, the logic of a system that refuses to recognize social inequality has no other way to explain inequality except by "those arising from individual gifts" (1979, p. 67).

Thus, leadership is a genetic capacity and not an acquired capability, which we call in this report an "accoutrement" (Papa & English, 2011). Khurana (2002) has identified the same thing when corporate searches look over the charismatic CEO and "believe that the charisma that they seek in candidates is something that comes through inheritance and early formative experiences and cannot be learned or acquired later in life" (p. 153).

Critics of candidates in traditional educational administration programs take the same approach. They argue that leaders lead through their "gifts" by using words that convey inborn and genetic capacities such as "talent," "attributes," "traits," "endowments," and "capabilities" (Thomas B. Fordham Institute & Broad Foundation, 2003). Khurana cites similar words in business, such as "chemistry," "executive presence," "articulation," "stature," and "change agent" (2002, p. 153).

With this ideology of charisma at the forefront, one needs minimal preparation, and the Broad Foundation's superintendent's academy ensures its candidates will fit by radically deskilling leadership positions, which "demonstrates" that formal preparation is unnecessary (English, 2004). The bottom line is that leaders are born and not prepared, and the main task is simply to find them.

However, Khurana points out dramatically that the so-called war for talent is a myth because it ignores the fact that in order for leaders to be successful, many others are required to assist them, and he notes, "No single individual can save an organization" (2002, p. 209).

No more high-level example could be found than Mayor Michael Bloomberg's appointment of Catherine Black, a person Bloomberg had called a "superstar manager in the private sector" and the First Lady of magazines, to the role of chancellor of the New York City schools (Martinez & Saul, 2011, p. A3). Black, a former publishing magnate manager, lasted all of ninety-five days on the job. A non-educator, her short term was marked by the departure of two deputy chancellors and "nearly half of the city's top education officials . . . since [her] appointment" (Halbfinger, 2011, p. A20). Black was replaced by an educator.

However, the idea that licensing or experience in education is unnecessary is a familiar one to the neoliberal agenda and is not confined to education. For example, it is now being argued that the practice of law should be "deregulated" and that the control of entry to the law profession via law schools and the American Bar Association should be changed because it would make legal services cheaper and create more jobs (Winston & Crandall, 2011).

The neoliberal argument is that "allowing accounting firms, management consulting firms, insurance agencies, investment banks and other entities to offer legal services would undoubtedly generate innovations in such services and would force existing law firms to change their way of doing business and to lower prices" (Winston & Crandall, p. A13). As in the attack on leadership preparation in schools of education, it is argued that competition for law services would lead to "a search for more efficient methods to serve clients" (p. A13).

Bourdieu (1998) has called this argument a "fatalistic doctrine" because

[it] gives itself the air of a message of liberation, through a whole series of lexical tricks around the idea of freedom, liberation, deregulation, etc. a whole series of euphemisms or ambiguous uses of words—"reform" for example—designed to present a restoration as a revolution, in a logic which is that of all conservative revolutions. (p. 50)

Neoliberals try to pass off their ideology as "common sense" without admitting that it is simply their point of view, and they rarely acknowledge their hidden agenda of imposing the "for-profit" mind-set on public services.

CONTINUING THE ACHIEVEMENT GAP DEBATE, WHICH IGNORES SOCIAL INEQUALITIES (1, 2)

The achievement gap that exists in American education will continue to be described as (a) a failure of schools to impact student performance, and/or (b) the genetic incapacity of some students in the public schools (Hernstein & Murray, 2004), and/or (c) a failure of leadership (see Sparks, 2011). What has been totally missing from this discussion is the relationship of achievement to social inequality. Bourdieu and Passeron (1979) speak to this eloquently:

Blindness to social inequalities both obliges and allows one to explain all inequalities, particularly with those in educational achievement, as natural inequalities, unequal giftedness. Such an attitude is part of the logic of a system which is based on the postulate of the formal equality of all pupils, as a precondition of its operation, and cannot recognize any inequalities other than those arising from individual gifts. (p. 67)

Social inequality is primarily an inequality of wealth, education, and economic privilege. This point is missed by the "reformers," who fail to understand that the achievement gap is connected to a wealth inequality gap, and so-called reforms that miss this point are not likely to make a serious dent in the gap, let alone erase it anytime soon (Rotberg, 2011).

When Condron (2011) examined the 2006 PISA data, he found a relationship between nations with large inequality gaps and lower test scores and observed that "highly inegalitarian affluent countries such as the United States could boost average student achievement by reducing income inequality" and that "high inequality is bad for everyone, not just those at the bottom" (p. 54).

The *Economist* ("Economics Focus," 2011) observed that the wealth gap in the United States, the largest in the world by many accounts (Irvin, 2008), was due in part to antipathy toward using taxation as a means to create a social safety net. The *Economist* article also noted a report by the OECD (Organisation for Economic Co-operation and Development) that taxation in America constitutes less than 30 percent of the average American's total compensation, compared to "50% in Germany and France" (p. 74). In a similar vein:

> Unsurprisingly, the American state is also less generous to the poor. Unemployment benefits in the United States replace a smaller share of income, and run out more quickly, than in most European countries. (p. 74)

One of the reasons that attitudes in the United States fail to see economic disparity as a causative agent in educational attainment is that social homogeneity, or *social cohesion*, plays a part in the notion of taking greater care of those at the bottom of the socioeconomic hierarchy.

> Broadly speaking, countries that are more ethnically or racially homogeneous are more comfortable with the state seeking to mitigate inequality by transferring some resources from richer to poorer people through the fiscal system. ("Economics Focus," 2011, p. 74)

One of the key factors is the extent to which those at the bottom of the socioeconomic ladder are immigrants.

The implications of understanding the connection between wealth and educational achievement is so far absent in many of the approaches imposed on schools that fail to demonstrate better test scores and the reduction of the achievement gap. After a meta-analysis of the relationship between socioeconomic status and academic achievement, Sirin said, "Thus, to significantly reduce the gap in achievement between low- and high-SES students, policy decisions at the local, state, and federal levels must aim at leveling the playing field for students deemed to be at risk academically as a result of their family SES" (2005, p. 446).

THE DEBASEMENT OF EDUCATION DEGREES AND PREPARATION BY ONLINE DIPLOMA MILLS (1, 2)

Online degrees by programs that require no qualifications or prior experiences in schools except for the necessary funds to pay for course work, and that lack both qualified faculty and an internship experience, where "face to face contact becomes anachronistic" and "deep engagement with critical educational issues is replaced with workbooks students can complete at their convenience" (Fusarelli, 2004, p. 29), have proliferated.

Papa and English (2010) found in a review of 1,027 doctoral dissertations completed during 2006–2008 as listed in ProQuest that "just under 20% of all Ph.D's in Educational Leadership are awarded by online/non-traditional universities" (p. 60). The *Chronicle of Higher Education* ("Student Demographics," 2011) reported that of twenty universities awarding the most doctorates in education in 2008–2009 (n = 2,667), five online for-profit universities awarded 966 of them for a total of 36 percent (p. 40).

The record of these programs is dismal. The for-profit online providers of college degrees have not improved the quality of higher education. Instead, they have driven quality to the bottom line.

For-profit higher education groups have paid millions of dollars back to the federal government for illegal recruiting techniques and other shady practices. Cary (2010) reports that "a quarter of all federal aid goes to for-profits, while they enroll only 10 percent of students" (p. A88).

Faculty at some of the for-profits speak of pressures on "employees to falsify attendance records, raise grades, and manipulate job-placement numbers" (Field, 2011, p. A1). An anonymous (2011) faculty member wrote in the *Chronicle of Higher Education*, "My four years of experience at a for-profit college revealed that the for-profit higher-education industry really is as corrupt as everyone suspects" (p. B12).

The *Economist* ("For-Profit Colleges," 2010) noted of the for-profits, "The industry is shrouded in fuzzy numbers. Reliable graduation rates and earnings data do not exist. More certain, however, is that the debt burden and default rates for graduates are particularly high. Critics claim that misleading recruiting lures students into programmes that leave them with heavy debt and flimsy skills" (p. 36). In fact, the average yearly tuition of a for-profit college in 2009 was $14,000, compared to $2,500 at a community college.

The culture of corruption across the full spectrum of the for-profit online degree mills puts the lie to the neoliberal claim that competition improves quality or reduces cost (Blumenstyk, 2004; Blumenstyk & Richards, 2011). And the public is not convinced of the efficacy of online courses. A national survey conducted by the Pew Research Center of 2,142 adults indicated that "[f]ewer than one-third of Americans believe that online college courses provide value equal to classroom instruction" (p. A8).

THE ESCALATING CULTURE OF NUMBERS AND CONTINUING CHEATING SCANDALS (1, 2)

To understand the sudden emergence of large test cheating scandals in Washington, DC, Atlanta, and elsewhere is to understand that normal teachers and administrators do not engage in such behavior if there are rational ways to reach reasonable objectives. The imposition of draconian, authoritarian, and punishment-centered managerial approaches, where all that counts is "mak[ing] your numbers" no matter what, has created an "approach to assessment and school leadership that is as damaging to the teaching profession as it is harmful to learning" (Powell, 2011, p. 25).

The development of widespread cheating and cooking-the-books antics coming into education is mirrored in the business world and in the "take no prisoners" attitude embodied in the famous Enron "rank and yank" system, in which employees were ranked against all others in a particular unit, and those of the bottom 10 percent fired (Fox, 2003, p. 83).

This "bell curve" model of management resulted in a cutthroat culture in which employees sabotaged the work of others, increased internal compartmentalization, and helped create an intensive interest in only short-term fixes. The competitive culture encouraged "a mercenary and selfish attitude" (Fox, 2003, p. 89).

When Yahoo! got into trouble and recently fired its fourth CEO within a few years, it brought in a so-called numbers guy to bring it back to profitability. The new CEO once joked to analysts that "Yahoo managers who don't make their numbers could be electrocuted at one of the company's data centers" (Letzing & Lublin, 2011, p. B4). Yet this is a company that critics charge "has failed at product innovation" (p. B4). If people are fearful for their jobs, they are unlikely to encourage radically new behavior and will instead stick to the tried and true, even if it doesn't work.

This "for-profit" business mind-set being forcefully advocated by so-called reformers has led to "a sense of spiritual bankruptcy within the corporate world" (Erdahl, 2010, p. 5). And in education, the cheating scandals that emerged from the business obsession with "numbers, numbers, numbers" is illustrative of that spiritual bankruptcy. For example, in Washington, DC, former chancellor Michelle Rhee began putting pressure on principals to improve test scores:

> According to Aona Jefferson, a former DC principal who is now president of the Council of Schools Officers . . . every year . . . Rhee met with each principal and asked what kind of test score gains he would post in the coming school year. Jefferson says principals told her that Rhee expected them to increase scores by 10 percentile points or more every year. "What do you do when your chancellor asks, 'How many points can you guarantee this year?'" Jefferson says, "How is a principal supposed to do that?" (Gillum & Bello, 2011, p. 5)

Michelle Rhee had no previous experience running a school system and later observed, "We weren't proactive and strategic enough about communication and thinking about how do we get out there and talk about the great things that are happening" (Aarons, 2010, p. 17).

Later, when the cheating scandal broke in DC, Rhee scoffed at the insinuations she had anything to do with it despite the fact that she had fired 241 teachers due to low student test scores (Banchero, 2010). Firing people over test score numbers is the ultimate threat to someone's notion of what is or what is not important.

Rhee and Beverly Hall, the former superintendent of Atlanta, both failed to publicly recognize that it is the superintendent of schools who establishes the climate of expectations and the tone of management for an organization. What people perceive as a survival task starts at the top with the setting of expectations. In Hall's case, her top administrative staff, consisting of four area superintendents and several school principals, were relieved from their duties. Her administrators reported that "they believed they would be ostracized if they did not deliver the results Dr. Hall wanted" (Severson, 2011).

An extensive state report detailed "widespread, systematic cheating by students, teachers and administrators" (Martin, 2011, p. A3). Hall took home nearly $600,000 in bonuses based on test score gains (Powell, 2011, p. 30). We foresee more cheating scandals in the future as unreasonable demands for instant "fix-its" based on test scores escalate, especially when they are used to evaluate and pay classroom teachers and educational administrators.

THE EROSION OF FULL-TIME TENURE-TRACK FACULTY IN OUR PREPARATION PROGRAMS (1, 2)

There has been a sea change in those working in higher education and in our programs. Schuster and Finkelstein (2006) highlight two distinctive shifts away from full-time, tenure-track appointments. The first is the creation of part-time faculty appointments for teaching-only purposes. The second is the creation of full-time employment on a fixed-term basis. Approximately one-fourth (7,800 of 32,200) of these full-time fixed-term faculty are "retirees" from a formerly full-time job. This statistic certainly applies to many preparation programs in a wide range of institutions.

One scary result is the creation of a *contingent workforce* in higher education. In fact, in some disciplines the majority of instructors constitute "collections of transients," even at research universities (Schuster & Finkelstein, 2006, p. 325). In 2009, between 13 percent and 50 percent of the academic workforce at public and private four-year institutions was part-time ("The Profession,"

2011), while "contingent or term appointments have become during the past decade the modal form of new full-time faculty appointments" (Schuster & Finkelstein, p. 324).

The growth in full-time non-tenure-track positions has been from 46 percent for public four-year institutions to 70 percent for private four-year institutions ("The Profession," 2011, p. 28). One result has been that "the research function for the most part has been limited to the work of the regular, full-time core faculty and has largely been squeezed out of the workload of those holding contingent appointments" (Schuster & Finkelstein, 2006, p. 325).

One of the consequences of a part-time or contingent workforce in our preparation programs is that it is increasingly centered on reproduction of the status quo, the endless repetition of strategies and work tasks to extend what exists into the future, even as rapid technological shifts and social inequalities demand changes in the content and scope of leadership roles in the schools.

Other negative trends identified by Schuster and Finkelstein include increased workload for a reduced core faculty; declining influence and power of the faculty within the institution; diminished institutional loyalty from faculty as they become more contingent and temporary workers; diminished protection of academic freedom and the role of larger social critique by the faculty; and increased polarization of institutions of higher education into teaching and training and those engaged in research (2006, pp. 342–43).

Finally, Schuster and Finkelstein ask the question, "At what point does an increasingly stratified institutional system begin 'disserving' the goals of human resource development and social mobility?" (p. 344).

Too often academic administrators are interested only in increased enrollments in educational leadership courses as the proverbial "cash cows" to keep other costs down. Coupled with transient faculty, the preparation of educational leaders takes on the form of a for-profit business model as opposed to a professional, academic model.

This trend is especially ominous as the once-dominant research-intensive educational leadership programs prepare the same number or fewer graduates, and there has been a pronounced shift toward smaller, more regional universities preparing leaders, especially at the doctoral levels (Baker, Orr, & Young, 2007). Whether doctoral research produced by these institutions can result in what Archbald (2008) calls work that results in "community benefit" by contributing new knowledge is a huge question with a largely transient faculty workforce forecast for mid-century.

The purpose of reviewing the "warning signs" is to oppose and/ or change them to move in the direction we believe is essential in order to reinvigorate our professional field and enable all schools to become more effective with the entire population of students, not just those who are now served well by them.

We propose actively opposing the developments in this chapter as it is clear that the trends cited are detrimental to the profession and to the preparation of educational practitioners.

Chapter Four

Leadership for Social Justice

This chapter focuses on fairness and poverty as a social justice issue specifically concerning not only the growing gap between rich and poor but also children living in poverty. The world requires a different type of leader, one who is committed to changing the impoverished conditions that affect schooling and the quality of life for children and youth alike. Here we do not write as utopian philosophers but rather as scholar-activists whose political views are grounded in data-based trends that will be operational for school communities at mid-century.

The deeply structured inequalities already existing in society bestow to some individuals much greater numbers of choices than others have. For Papa and English (2011), schools cannot be solely responsible for somehow compensating for the inequalities of life chances. These inequities are true for babies and are in full swing years before children ever start school.

Making social justice happen requires so much beyond schooling. The perspectives on such deep problems and solutions that best fit reside in the larger social structure and, paradoxically, the startling disparities embedded in it. The *mid-century leader*, therefore, will understand that schooling is just part of the equation in advancing the cause of *justice as fairness*.

The broader goal of equitable schooling and sound leadership for mid-century leaders is social justice. The journey to recognize this goal is familiarity with fairness. The common humanity of children requires explicit actions that are earmarked by a common good for all. Progress may be uneven. The pace and scope of the change required sets us on a path of universalism, born from political decisions that yield fairness in action.

As the educational leaders of today, we must anticipate with confidence a better future for all children, and we remain steadfastly hopeful and expectant. The inabilities of today have not achieved Rawls's (1971) moral evaluation of social and political perspectives. Rawls believes that in a just society the liberties of equal citizenship are grasped. These rights secured by justice are simply not subject to political pandering of social interests.

Fairness is unambiguous yet complex to achieve. To act in fairness is a moral journey achieved by conscious thought and action. All persons are created equal, said President Lincoln in his Gettysburg Address: "Four score and seven years ago our fathers brought forth on this continent, a new nation, conceived in Liberty, and dedicated to the proposition that all men are created equal" (Bartlett, 1968, p. 639).

From Lincoln's sense of equality and liberty, the roadmap to Rawls is clear. Or is it? Rawls determines the extent of social justice based on two principles. The first is that "each person is to have an equal right to the most extensive basic liberty compatible with a similar liberty for others"; the second is that "social and economic inequalities are to be arranged so that they are both (a) reasonably expected to be to everyone's advantage, and (b) attached to positions and offices open to all" (1971, p. 60).

The evolution from these principles is that the very structure of the larger society is part and parcel of a perspective on social justice (Papa & English, 2011).

From an ethical perspective, fairness involves issues of equality, impartiality, proportionality, openness, and due process, according to Josephson. Applying these principles in daily life is quite difficult due to the complexity of life's real issues. Essentially, "fairness implies adherence to a balanced standard of justice without reference to one's own biases or interests" (Josephson, 2002, p. 12). Translating Josephson's ethical considerations into Rawls's concept of fairness takes the discourse up a notch to a more unequivocal level: fairness in action.

How equal rights and open access are provided has implications for the United States. International student comparisons on US student performance have recently found solid research with Condron (2011), who argues that a strong connection exists between economic inequality and educational achievement in affluent societies. His analyses of data from the 2006 Programme for International Student Assessment (PISA) and other sources indicate that "egalitarian countries have higher average achievement, higher percentages of very highly skilled students and lower percentages of very low-skilled students than do less egalitarian countries" (p. 47).

Why do the affluent US students underperform students from other affluent countries? To date, comparisons have focused on the educational system. Researchers have not focused on what Condron believes to be most relevant: the United States is the most *economically unequal* affluent country. His study, which explored the relationship between economic inequality and student achievement in affluent countries, found that "highly inegalitarian affluent countries such as the U.S. could boost average student achievement by reducing income inequality" (p. 51). Culprits perpetuating widespread injustice named by him include those listed below:

1. Child poverty
2. Health disparities among children
3. A higher degree of racial/ethnic heterogeneity and inequality
4. School resource inequality (p. 53)

How problematic is it for schools to serve as *the great equalizer* (Johnson, 2006)? In this book, we have argued that schools alone cannot reverse achievement disparities. The mid-century leader will hopefully live in a country where the root of inequality is transformed because it will have been addressed more forcefully.

Poverty, according to the World Bank, is "pronounced deprivation in well-being . . . low incomes . . . inability to acquire basic goods and services necessary for survival with dignity . . . and encompasses low levels of health, education . . . clean water and sanitation, inadequate physical security, and lack of voice" (2005, p. 1). The emotional dimension manifests as insufficient opportunities to better one's life.

Poverty is difficult to define (Dougherty, 2011). The complexity rests in the divergence of peoples, who they are, where they come from, and where they live. Jolliffe (2004) identifies six types of poverty, stated here:

1. *Situational poverty* is generally caused by a sudden crisis or loss, and is often temporary. Events causing situational poverty include environmental disasters, divorce, or severe health problems.
2. *Generational poverty* occurs in families where at least two generations have been born into poverty. Families living in this type of poverty are not equipped with the tools to move out of their situations.
3. *Absolute poverty*, which is rare in the United States, involves a scarcity of such necessities as shelter, running water, and food. Families who live in absolute poverty tend to focus on day-to-day survival.
4. *Relative poverty* refers to the economic status of a family whose income is insufficient to meet its society's average standard of living.

5. *Urban poverty* occurs in metropolitan areas with populations of at least fifty thousand people. The urban poor deal with a complex aggregate of chronic and acute stressors (including crowding, violence, and noise) and are dependent on often-inadequate large-city services.

6. *Rural poverty* occurs in nonmetropolitan areas with populations below fifty thousand. In rural areas, there are more single-guardian households, and families often have less access to services, support for disabilities, and quality education opportunities.

Such trends as stated above suggest these questions: What roles do and will schools have in addressing poverty? How much equity, and to what populations or situations? The mid-century leader will have to understand complexities surrounding poverty, equity, and family vulnerability to achieve schools that are socially just for all students.

What, then, falls outside of schools' circumference of influence now and even in the future? Schools and those who lead them do not influence broad social realities, such as the tax structure of the state or the bankruptcy issues relative to housing or transportation needs. Global realities include access to water, buffering of natural disasters, and financial debacles such as the *great recession* (2007–2014) that have a devastating economic effect worldwide.

THROUGH NO FAULT OF THEIR OWN

The 2005 census data on income, poverty, and health insurance coverage in the United States indicated that "nearly 18 percent of children under age 18 . . . live in poverty and children comprise one-third of all people living in poverty [in the United States]"

(Marshall & Oliva, 2010, p. 60). The poverty rate among blacks is 24.9 percent and among Hispanics, 21.8 percent, while for Asians it is 11 percent and for whites, 8.3 percent.

How poverty is defined is challenging to detect. Barry (2005) states that poverty as defined in practice during the 1960s was family income that was less than three times the cost of low-priced food. This number was based on the premise that families spend a third of their income on food. Barry contends that if the poverty index were updated to today, it would take 50 percent more above the current level: "The failure to maintain even the purchasing power of the 1960s as the criterion of poverty is a grim reminder of the political invisibility of the poor in the United States" (p. 172).

The reality is that children who live in the United States depend on local and state revenues for many health and social services, including public schooling. Yet the national interest is for a healthy and well-educated future workforce (Golden, Macomber, & Harwood, 2008). For the most part, metropolitan areas that are child-rich largely consist of immigrant families. And nationally, "more than one in four (28%) children of immigrants live in *linguistically isolated* households, where no adult speaks English very well. . . . [For] these immigrant children . . . [there is a] need to spend more on education to ensure that all children succeed in school" (p. 1).

What, then, might be the trends to prognosticate? With uninhibited abandon, the following are proffered.

Trend 1: Prognosticating the Demographics of 2050

The national goal for schooling is for all children to have the opportunity to reach their full potential as productive adults (Popkin, Acs, & Smith, 2010). Where children live geographically largely determines their life chances.

High-poverty neighborhoods are subjected to extreme levels of racial and economic segregation. Popkin and colleagues also found that inadequate public services (police, grocery stores, etc.) lead to a range of negative outcomes, such as poor physical and mental health, gang activities, delinquency, teen parents, and so on. These researchers urge that data at the local and national levels need unpacking so that we can learn "how place affects development, health, and risky behavior for children and youth" (p. 2).

The elderly receive more financial aid from federal sources than any other population group. And, since the late 1960s, poverty for the elderly has greatly worsened. The National Policy Center (2006) reports that poverty differs across subgroups, citing great variation between racial and ethnic groups, single black or Hispanic women who head houses, and native-born versus foreign-born families:

- Poverty rates for blacks and Hispanics greatly exceed the national average. In 2009, 25.8 percent of blacks and 25.3 percent of Hispanics were poor, compared with 9.4 percent of non-Hispanic whites and 12.5 percent of Asians.
- In 2009, 29.9 percent of households headed by single women were poor, while 16.9 percent of households headed by single men and 5.8 percent of married-couple households lived in poverty.
- In 2009, 19.0 percent of foreign-born residents lived in poverty, compared with 13.7 percent of residents born in the United States. Foreign-born noncitizens had an even higher incidence of poverty, at a rate of 25.1 percent (p. 1).

So this leads us to the question, how many children in the United States actually live in poverty? The National Policy Center report found that "children represent a disproportionate share of the poor . . . 25 percent of the total population, but 35 percent of the poor population. . . . In 2008, 15.45 million children, or 20.7 percent, were poor" (p. 3). No doubt about it—the reality of children living in poverty is exacerbated by race and Hispanic origin.

USA Today (Nasser, 2008) reports that the Hispanic population will triple by 2050 based on projections released by the Pew Research Center. The US population will grow to 438 million from 303 million. Additionally:

- Nearly one in five Americans will have been born outside the United States versus one in eight in 2005. Sometime between 2020 and 2025, the percentage of foreign-born will surpass the historic peak reached a century ago during the last big immigration wave. New immigrants and their children and grandchildren born in the United States will account for 82 percent of the population increase from 2005 to 2050.
- Whites who are not Hispanic, now two-thirds of the population, will become a minority when their share drops to 47 percent. They made up 85 percent of the population in 1960.
- Hispanics, already the largest minority group, will more than double. (p. 1)

Fifty years ago there was no *Hispanic* term designated by demographers. As whites become the new minority, the current designations of race and ethnicity will change, but how? Will the designation "non-Hispanic white" be the label used for the new minority? Not likely, as our sense of fairness would not label any race/ethnicity as "non."

Poverty is static and unchanging. In other words, despite all of the changes affecting families, what is not improving is poverty and the conditions within which children are born and youth inherit. Barry states, "[A] new-born baby cannot possibly be responsible for the material social conditions into which it is born, and . . . whatever *decisions* a child may make for a number of years after that cannot be its responsibility" (2005, p. 46). Individual responsibility, the present political focus, avoids local, state, and federal responsibility.

Trend 2: Social Justice as Ubiquitous in Practice

To prognosticate is to "forecast or predict something future from present indications or signs" (Dictionary.com, 2011, p. 1). To believe that forty years henceforth poverty will be eradicated is wishful thinking.

Though the present truth holds opposite meaning to this, mid-century schools can be those "sacred" places where there is serious questioning of the social order. Barry (2005) describes current conditions where the political wave of state responsibility translates into a judgment that if schools are poor, it is because of the poor choices within them (as opposed to those made on behalf of them by outsiders, such as policymakers).

One can envision that all public school parents of 2050 will be considered "customers" who are able to "shop around" for schools that meet their children's specific needs. During the first two decades of the twenty-first century, charter schools acted as filters that kept the best students, relegating the mediocre students and their families to public schools. As customers in 2050, the ease of helping parents decide on a school will be due to social networking.

Mid-century school leaders are clearly levers of social change (Barry, 2005), whereas in 2011 the "blame the victim" mentality becomes utterly unacceptable. Failures from the early decades of the twenty-first century made the truth vibrantly known that poverty had to be addressed, not ignored.

School leaders of the future will have learned from some of our past mistakes as a civilization. With the population shifts, such as the Hispanic growth in numbers of school-age children, coupled with the rapidly developing technological tools, social networks, and so on, public schools may indeed serve as a societal influence.

Lack of information that mirrors parents and poverty will foster better-informed parents. Limitations in perspective and mistakes made in the first and second decade of this century will be addressed, such as a greater understanding of parents' unequal resources, described in 2005 as qualifications, and pay of those who provide child care—how well a child is fed, school attendance problems, and so forth. With solutions envisioned, Barry stated, "children lose out if their parents cannot afford to take time off to look after them when they are sick or deal with crises. This requires paid leave for parents" (p. 54).

What prevents school leaders today from being able to show success for all students? Is part of the answer found in what educational researchers do? Barry (2005) questions why, if we pursue social justice, intensive research efforts have not been devoted to find the best ways to overcome the disadvantages children come to school with and "continue to suffer from—as a consequence of their home and neighborhood environment" (p. 55).

The mid-century school leader will be working in an era of changing environments and conditions in which children are born. As learning for children becomes more specialized to each student, the school leader's role expands into working within the community in ways that ensure social services are available to students and their families on or adjacent to the school site. School choice, the noted panacea earlier this century, will have clarified for state and federal leaders that choice alone was not the answer.

Life chances for children and their families, if not improved, will entrench current barriers to success. Stated in the affirmative, they will lead to a successful schooling experience that gives the nation the global, educated worker desired. Barry forecast a roadmap for altering the injustices, stating that political processes need to disturb the cycle "by which the advantages of one generation are transmitted to the next" (2005, p. 69).

Past and current thought constructs a reality surrounding the dominant school culture that is neither neutral nor universal. The question of elites and marginalized devolves from state and federal levels. Barry aptly summarized this sociopolitical hegemony:

> In every society, the prevailing belief system has been largely
> created by those with the most power—typically, elderly males
> belonging to the majority ethnic and religious group, who also
> run the dominant institutions of society. (p. 27)

Barry's perspective from 2005 will be dramatically altered as more
women will move into roles of power in schools. Between 1993
and 1994, and 2003 and 2004, the percentage of public school
principals who were female increased from 41 to 56 percent in
elementary schools and from 14 to 26 percent in secondary schools
(National Center for Education Statistics, 2011, p. 1).

This role of the school in defining the only legitimate version of
reality open to its young is an example of Bourdieu and Passeron's
(2000) "cultural arbitrary." No culture is "natural," but they usually
appear to be so to those within them (Papa & English, 2011). As
Levin states:

> The quest for educational equity is a moral imperative for a
> society in which education is a crucial determinant of life
> chances. Yet whether there is an economic return to the taxpayer
> for investing in educational justice is often not considered.
> (2009, p. 5)

Mid-century leaders will know that to stop inequities, we must not
punish students for being poor and not having access to the forms
of cultural capital that children from more advantaged homes already possess. These leaders will have learned that blaming children living in poverty for their "lack of cultural knowledge" is
wrong. Cultural differences are the norm.

The excesses discovered during the *great recession* from 2007
to 2009 (Goldman, 2009) brought to light abuses in business and
banking. In 1998, the average CEO compensation was 419 times
the pay of the average blue-collar worker, but by 2003 it had become 531 times the average. The egregious inequities perpetuated
by these business leaders have drawn the ire of Congress and even

many in the business, media, educational, and wider community, but there is no relief on the horizon (Useem, 2003). The 24/7 news format has today encouraged Comedy Central comedians to use the Socratic search for truth in politics.

In fact, the *great recession* really is not expected to stop hurting middle- and low-income families until around 2014–2015. The economic determinants of deciding that it ended in 2009 are meaningless to families in poverty, as these families in high numbers remain poor.

Trend 3: Fairness for All

As we approach 2050, the definition of social justice as fairness as advanced by Rawls is likely to have some airplay in the definition and encompassing of individual student/family practices. When *fairness* is examined, it has to first be considered outside of the school (Papa & English, 2011). The mid-century leader has to understand not only how the internal mechanisms within a school work against the poor but also how the poor are positioned in the larger social structure before their children ever even arrive in the school. In Rawls's own words:

> The primary subject of justice is the basic structure of society or more exactly, the way in which the major social institutions distribute fundamental rights and duties and determine the division of advantages from social cooperation. . . . The major institutions [such as schools] define men's rights and duties and influence their life prospects, what they can expect to be and how well they can hope to do. (1971, p. 7)

WHAT WE ARE BECOMING, WE *ARE* AS A NATION

The mid-century leader will likely understand that to be fair one must be intellectually curious in seeking solutions and caring for the practices within the school (Papa, 2011b). Curiosity regarding poverty, as a character aspect of the school leader, can be construed as an action of fairness as it asks "why" with no assigning of blame. The effects of cumulative advantage (and likewise disadvantage) are why educators, when they practice social justice through fairness of intent, through actions, and through practices, are vital for the mid-century leader to recognize.

As Barry (2005) foretold, the perpetuation of cumulative inequality is a form of determinism. This determinism found in social services is political in origin: "The range of political interests . . . mobilized . . . to disturb the process by which the advantages of one generation are transmitted to the next" (p. 69).

Fairness in intent and action is social justice. The sense of basic liberty for all means similar liberty for me and for others. Rawls, preceded by Lincoln (Bartlett, 1968), asks not only for a sense of similar liberty but also for one coupled with social and economic equalities so that everyone is advantaged and all avenues of everyday life are open to all.

What we know about poverty is that early childhood interventions can counter poverty's impact. Jensen (2009) believes that to limit the impact of poverty, the staff at the school must have great understanding of the children and families and the community they live in, and the school leader must expect empathy from the school staff, not pity.

Understanding the situations of poverty is democracy in action. Condron's research clearly displays that egalitarian societies "do not have fewer very highly skilled students" (2011, p. 54). He embraces the idea, the promise as we see it, that "creating a more egalitarian economic system might help improve . . . U.S. students' skills."

In chapter 1 we tackled the subject of the contested times in which we live today. The meanness of the rhetoric found in the current 24/7 news as platitudes has caused the schools to despair.

The mid-century leader we have called the Net Gener will, in 2050, have figured out our sad predicament of inequities from forty years earlier and will have embraced an image based on a fairness of practice and heart that, we think, should bring to the fore willful promise followed by practices that will affect children's predicaments and their future for the better. Rawls knew fairness would put us on the utopian road. That is the dream, found in the actions of fairness.

Part III

Promises

Why cannot a teacher be a leader and exercise leadership on his/her own terms? Why cannot a teacher have a vision and mission for his/her classroom, and have his/her own development agenda? In the current policy context it seems that teachers cannot be allowed to exercise leadership in this way as it would disrupt the power structures that are historically and socially located, and consequently teachers are unable to support pupils as leader learners.

—Helen M. Gunter (2002), *Leaders and Leadership in Education* (p. 127)

Chapter Five

Accoutrements: Connecting the Art and Science of Leadership

This chapter paints a picture of what leadership would be about if we were successful in creating a more socially just notion of schooling and if we were able to combine the art and science of the study of leadership.

The promise is that school would be more inclusive; we would not see the extreme and growing disparities in material wealth; resegregation occurring in charter schools and in policies that result in resegregation would be seen as morally wrong.

This setting described above has been the focus for this report. Schools cannot nor should not right all wrongs in society, but they should not be used to perpetuate a status quo that continues the tradition of inequality between the "haves" and "have-nots" that is the largest in the world. Such wealth disparities constitute a severe threat to democracy. This chapter concentrates on what within schools the mid-century leader should aspire to be.

THE ACCOUTREMENTS NECESSARY FOR THE 2050 LEADER

The professional educational leadership standards of today present the school leader with learned skills derived from a behavioral science perspective. This worldview has a long history in our field and continues to hold sway over how we envision leadership to be constructed. But it also has well-documented shortcomings. It is only one lens of many to examine leadership. We contend these skills are *the floor* for the school leader. These skills are primarily predicated on a patina of research and a large dose of craft knowledge (Papa & English, 2011).

Papa and English have described *the floor* of leadership training as being tied to federal and state standards. These standards, known today as core knowledge or common core, tend to be skill and content specific. The standards are presented as invariate across schools, districts, or geographic location, urban, rural, and suburban. The skills are to be lodged into courses and acquired through training and intern experiences for potential principals and superintendents.

Beyond basic skill and content acquisition is what Papa (2011b) calls the accoutrements a leader needs to possess. The acquisition of the accoutrements enables leaders to grow and become more effective over time. The accoutrements were developed from an extensive review of the literature and a decade of empirical and scholarly data gathering, which included *Leadership on Purpose: Promising Practices for African American and Hispanic Students* (Papa & Fortune, 2002) and other recent studies of successful schools and the leaders found in them (Papa & English, 2011).

The sources for these accoutrements are shown in figure 5.1. It is important to note that, unlike lists of skills employed to describe leaders that rest on assumptions we find deeply problematic (such as the supposition that one generic set of skills is good for all times, places, and possible situations, which thus rests on a false base of social intractability and contextual invariance), we posit that leaders are engaging in leadership work in a dynamic and fluid environment in which, as John Keegan (1987) remarked, "context is everything" (p. 3).

Leading Adult Learners

John Rawls (1971) defines social justice as *fairness* and says that it reflects the idea that "justice is the basic structure of society . . . the way in which the major social institutions distribute fundamental rights and duties and determine the division of advantages from social cooperation" (p. 7). Fairness in actions toward all staff, students, and parents makes a socially just school.

Leaders should know adult learners learn on a need-to-know basis (Papa & Papa, 2011). Teacher professional development must be anchored on adult learning principles. If we know how learners approach the acquisition of knowledge, then we can arrange strategies that will enhance their learning. Fairness for the adult learner takes the learner at his/her particular learning point. All profession-

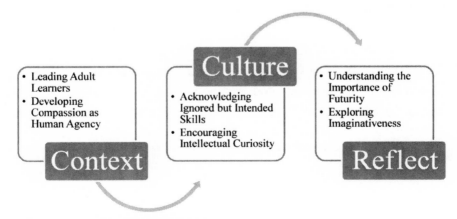

Figure 5.1. The Accoutrements

al development for teachers and principals is based on how each individual learner learns. For example, in the shaping of culture for the adult learner,

> Principals and the superintendent undergo the same professional development as the teachers with respect to instructional tools. During those two days of each week, the superintendent doesn't involve the principals in administration, except in emergencies.

Developing Compassion as Human Agency

English (2008, 2009) describes postmodernism as realism through *textual deconstruction* of the "overzealous reliance on scientific based structure that brings privilege to class, gender, sexual identity, and race-based social/cultural differentiated structure" (p. xxv). From this perspective, the restoration of human agency is described as follows:

> The idea that one individual human being is important and can bring about change in human life, in society, and in organizations such as schools, means also returning to an inclusive view of the role of culture, language, values and mythology in examining the importance of leaders in society and in schools. (English & Papa, 2010, p. 25)

We know that one-size-fits-all systems do not work. The totality of our students' mental, physical, and spiritual aspects is the package that must be taken into perspective. How better to understand human agency? We must ensure the future school leader has a varied repertoire of fair, ethical, and just behaviors. For example, in the shaping of culture as compassion in human agency:

> They are encouraged and supported to build personal relationships with their students, staffs and parents to make it easier and more productive in the work environment.

Acknowledging Ignored but Intended Skills

Eisner defined *ignored but intended skills*. Cognition takes shape through one's senses and consciousness (2005, pp. 76–77). The functions of the senses are described as crucial:

> They [teachers] bring to awareness the qualitative world we inhabit. To become aware of the world, two conditions must be satisfied. First, the qualities must be available for experiencing by a sentient human being. Second, the individual must be able to *read* their presence. When both of these conditions are met, the human being is capable of forming concepts of the world. These concepts take shape in the information that the senses have provided. (p. 77)

Heifetz (1994) believes leadership requires "listening as a trial and error process of making an interpretation, seeing where it falls short, and revising it. To listen, one has to live with doubt" (p. 271). So listening is a two-way street for the leader.

How do we measure a good listener? How are we trained in observation? We know it is vital for the socially just *activist* leader to be caring and fair. Vision building requires it. Strong personnel relations demand it and have the understanding that it is okay and normal to wrestle with complex issues. For example, the shaping of culture focuses on ignored but intended skills:

> At district meetings the superintendent listens and observes the communication emphasized with each administrative team member sharing assessments of his/her school, using data to talk about achievement, student issues, parent issues, and so on.

Encouraging Intellectual Curiosity

A curious leader is always searching for answers. Schally (2006) tells us that "an effective leader must be constantly asking the right questions," as curiosity is "a passion for discovery that appears to be hardwired in all of us—a primal instinct. As leaders, how curious are we about our stakeholders, our suppliers, our products' value, our competition, our position in the marketplace, our own personal growth potential?" (p. 1). Goodwin and Ristvey (2011) believe that by tapping into a student's natural curiosity, more interesting lessons will develop. Encouraging teachers to own *their curiosity* begs for a leader who understands curiosity.

A leader is curious. We can prepare school leaders to be curious about their school setting. Curiosity in learning and how it is fostered in the school environment is critical for school staff to develop, understand, and apply. Curiosity is fairness in action, as it asks "why" with no assigning of blame. It ensures that student achievement data, teacher evaluations, principal evaluations, and district evaluations are prepared in a setting of rational inquisitiveness about compelling questions. For example, in the shaping of culture, in order for the school leader to exhibit intellectual curiosity,

> Principals are encouraged by their superintendent to seek literature on relevant topics and provide budgets to explore alternative solutions to student learning outcomes.

Understanding Futurity

Leaders must be exposed to learning frames that go against the grain of current wisdom (Papa & Fortune, 2002; Papa, 2011a). Technology tools confer on us a false sense that it should be easier to solve the problems we face within our schools than it really is while providing supposed efficiencies. And we now know that when problems become too difficult, students can move on to charter or for-profit schools, leaving behind public schools.

Going against the grain may just be the best leader trait we can encourage. Futurity in action demands that a school leader anticipate what trend may come next. For example, in the shaping of culture, for the leader to understand the need for futurity,

The superintendent and principal focus is on where they are now, where they want to go, and what trends are coming that they can embrace.

Exploring Imaginativeness

Elliot Eisner had this to say about *imagination*: "Our imaginative life is built out of experience . . . [and] one would think, given the importance of imagination, that it would be regarded as one of the basics of education" (2005, p. 108). He also wrote that culture depends on communication. The accoutrements are what we, the authors, believe are important to be acknowledged and embraced, so that

> [t]he nuances and pleasures of a Beethoven quartet are experienced; the differences between a smile and a smirk are noticed; the achievements of a fine craftsman are appreciated. It is through a cultivated and refined sensibility that patterns in nature and culture are distinguished. It is from these patterns that the works of science and art are built. (p. 107)

Creativity, inspiration, originality, resourcefulness, visionary, artistic, inventive, and *ingenious* are synonyms for *imaginative leadership*. A good heart; an almost spiritual need to be of service for others; to be the hope for others; to help others be all they can be; to see the good in others—these qualities are all limited only by one's lack of imagination. For example, in the shaping of culture by the leader who understands the importance of imaginativeness,

> Principals spend two days a week as instructional leader, visible in classrooms and active in instruction. And, especially in times such as economic downturns and the condemnation of public schools, they provide hope to ensure everybody's *bucket is full* instead of empty.

Imagination, according to Maxine Greene, is what makes empathy possible, "for it is what helps us understand alternative realities" (Collins & O'Brien, 2003, p. 174). The mid-century leader embraces the qualitative aspects (Eisner, 2005) and moves forward steered by curiosity and imagination.

These essential *accoutrements* are the most important bits and pieces that are the earmark of a great school leader (Papa, 2011b) at mid-century. This is leadership beyond managerial tasks and standards measured. It has been said that one can be a good manager but not necessarily a good leader. This is a false dichotomy, for that it can be argued that good leaders need the basics of management for the leadership qualities to be exhibited (English, 2008, p. 13).

Intentional development of these characteristics does separate the great from the good leader. Accoutrements are leadership characteristics that are not explicitly taught in training programs but should be. This can only happen when professors and other business enterprise models acknowledge these characteristics in creating an enlightened mid-century leader.

THE REVITALIZATION OF PUBLIC SCHOOLING

We think the mid-century leader will have to be a digitally attuned humanitarian who is equipped to contend with the proliferating challenges of tomorrow's schools. University-based preparation programs have a serious role to play with respect to preparing tomorrow's digital leaders.

Simultaneously, we need to change limited conceptions of diversity and technology in the NCATE/ELCC standards and our own curricula so that our teaching and mentoring give rise to mid-century leaders as social justice proponents. Diversity and learning technology will be cultural standards of excellence and equity for schooling environments. Critical policy decisions regarding diversity and technology have repercussions for all aspects of education (Creighton, 2011).

What will mid-century leadership be like in the digital age for leaders for whom the learning and success of youth from diverse backgrounds will be a global concern? They will be prepared to lead mid-century schools in the "learning in technology" era (Barnett & Archambault, 2010; Schrader, 2008). How might schools of education, school districts, and community agencies prepare for the challenges associated with a cultural-technological revolution that could promote learning and fairness (e.g., equity, excellence, success) for students and schools, as well as disrupt fairness?

Can we predict what jobs will be available in 2050? Is the global arena for workers able to be predicted for 2050? Will attitude and creativity trump job skill training for today when jobs are unpredictable for 2020? Do we educate for jobs only? Or do we prepare students for intended jobs while also educating them for activism within the moral framework of globalization, so that all will have access to clean water, safety from physical abuses, and so on? From Ralph Nader's 2008 platform, Spring wrote:

> Government should encourage schools to infuse their curriculum with civic experiences that teach students both how to connect classroom learning to the outside world and how to practice democracy. Empower students with the knowledge and tools needed to become a major reservoir of future democracy. (2010, p. 156)

Learning in technology is a new cultural standard of excellence and equity for schooling environments (Barnett & Archambault, 2010). This era is distinguishable from what we know today, yet we do not need to rely solely on predictions to imagine revolutionary changes in learning. In today's educational institutions, teachers and professors generally emphasize learning about technology, from technology, and with technology—all "modes" for which technology occupies its own domain.

In effect, we compartmentalize technology, treating it as a hinge for learning processes and outcomes. Schrader's analysis of this pervasive situation introduces the "learning in technology" concept, which necessitates a different mind-set about technology's role in the future. Learning in technology will be immersive, and learning contexts will be created where environments and students are "one," as Schrader puts it.

In such select high-powered, well-resourced environments, students' interactions within a virtual environment could be evaluated for learning using a variety of methods (e.g., analysis of server logs, ethnography constructions, etc.). Interactions could be conversations among "players," "users," or "characters" in which inquiries frame learning, promote decision-making, and capitalize on problem solving (Barnett & Archambault, 2010). Student teachers and prospective leaders could assess peer interactions and digital technologies so they understand how to foster high quality, inquiry explorations, including judgments that support critical thinking.

Creighton (2005) has stated, "If we continue to focus mostly on the surface, huge numbers of minority and at-risk students will continue to fall farther . . . out of the learning organization altogether" (p. 34).

Recent data released by the US Department of Agriculture reported that more than 17.2 million households in the United States suffered from "food insecurity," a near-record high last year (Pugh, 2011, p. 7A). "Food insecurity" is defined by the United States Department of Agriculture as "limited to uncertain availability of nutritionally adequate and safe foods" (p. 7A).

FUTURITY: WHO DO WE WANT TO BE IN 2050?

Public perception of education has changed from seeing it as a drain on state and federal resources to seeing it as a public good investment, both for the individual leading a happier and more productive life and for economic viability.

1. Student dropout rates have stopped by mid-century.
2. Schools are more student service–focused, with a broad curriculum that includes the arts and humanities as well as math and science.
3. Practices and the research supporting it are shared for tweaking to the *individual*, classroom, school, district differences.
4. Ending of poverty might be possible through the improvement of greater educational opportunity for all students and families.
5. Students work globally in fair and just ways: ethically, economically, socially, and politically.
6. The accoutrements of leadership earmark principal preparation.

We believe that one of the primary answers for children of poverty is early childhood opportunities to aid those who are not privileged. Support for the working family should be given in child care open to all children, from birth forward. Early childhood programs should also be for all children, especially affordable for those in poverty as strong investments for combating prisons and teen pregnancy.

The cycle of poverty is now a multinational concern so that all countries must be economically elevated. By using a human capital model, Nobel economist Heckman said that "after making a cost benefit analysis of many proposed school reforms [we] concluded that preschool education yielded the most financial returns for invested dollars" (Spring, 2010, p. 12). Studies show that children in early childhood education programs are more likely "to score higher in reading and math, more likely to graduate from high school and attend college, more likely to hold a job, and more likely to earn more in that job" (Spring, p. 17).

THE SPECTER OF PHILANTHROCAPITALISM

What is the American dream in 2050? Is it one of social mobility and hope for everyone? Who is marginalized in 2050? Jensen (2009) tells us that "chronic socioeconomic deprivation can create environments that undermine the development of self and the capacity for self-determination and self-efficacy" (p. 3). He continues to unfold the map of poverty:

> Common issues in low-income families include depression, chemical dependence, and hectic work schedules—all factors that interfere with the healthy attachments that foster children's self-esteem, sense of mastery of their environment, and optimistic attitudes. Instead, poor children often feel isolated and unloved, feelings that kick off a downward spiral of unhappy life events, including poor academic performance, behavioral problems, dropping out of school and drug abuse. These events tend to rule out college as an option and perpetuate the cycle of poverty. (p. 3)

The authors of this report have decided to be fearless in our predictions by acknowledging some very recent reports that are hopeful for public schools. Wood predicted twenty years ago that standardized tests would go away, charter schools would lead innovation to sweep the country, NCLB would be benign in its impact on schools, and funding lawsuits would resolve the horrific inequitable funding across schools.

None of this came to pass, for today schools in the United States are "some of the most unequally funded in the world" (Wood, 2011, p. 19). Wood offers hope for the future if we heed and reverse these trends: international comparisons should make the United States aware that what happens in the classroom and *outside the classroom* is highly important, such as poor health care, unsafe neighborhoods, and so on; the assessment *craze* that leads to the need for cheaper and easier tests to measure student achievement, which absolutely dumbs down the curriculum, must reverse itself; and the public, through policymakers, must acknowledge that the public education system is central to the higher good of the United States.

Tirozzi (2011) believes that the federal direction allowing alternate principal certifications "that remove the pesky technical restriction of *teaching experience*" (p. 2) are wrong. Why is this wrong? Tirozzi notes lack of credibility with teachers and the possibility that the least qualified leaders will land in the highest-need schools.

The school reform path may be already changing away from the folly of nationalized curricula dumbed down to match cheap and easy assessments. Site-level leadership is the most effective leadership, a fact with which we can all agree. Melendez de Santa Ana (2011) believes local efforts with principals leading the way in small schools and a personalized student focus is the way to achieve true reform. We offer a more radical view in the last chapter with the concept of a *pedagogically centered* perspective of an educational leader.

Ravitch (Umphrey, 2011), in a recent interview, speaks to her complete turnaround position that now supports public education. She believes, first, that the push to primarily prepare students for college, not for life, is muting the role of public education. Second, charter schools have not fulfilled their promise of being incubators of innovation because they have been contrasted with failing public schools as saviors of the system. Finally, the greed of corporate America needs to be questioned as it pursues a path of power and influence challenging the historical democracy known as public education.

Ravitch's interview concludes with the following statement:

> This is a time for resolve, a time for professionalism, a time to defend public education against its detractors, a time to support the education profession from those who dismantle it and a time to stand up for what we know is right for students and for our society. (Umphrey, 2011, p. 36)

Examples of Ravitch's last point abound. The Bill and Melinda Gates Foundation, the Eli Broad Foundation, and the Walton Family Foundation offer strong evidence to support her contention. As cash-strapped poor K–20 public institutions look for ways to survive and perform effectively on behalf of all students, who among them will turn down a monetary grant that feeds the pockets of the for-profit sides of these foundations? So when the Gates Foundation gives money to transform schools' use of technology (Bill Gates's company technology), is this truly altruistic?

The extreme power of these foundations to influence the national and state agenda is unparalleled in public education history. The demand from them to adopt forced market-based policies on public education is indisputable. Umphrey terms this political force *philanthrocapitalism* (2011).

A rejection of the philanthrocapitalism approach can be found in a recent nationwide survey of school board members. Samuels (2011) reports that the market-based policies, such as charter schools, merit pay for teachers, school choice, privatization, recruiting nontraditional teachers, and so on, "are not as important to student achievement as strong leadership, both at the building site and district level and professional development" (p. 1). Additionally, this survey of nine hundred school board members, twelve hundred superintendents, and more than five hundred school districts across the nation shows that the participants believe that the number one goal of education is to "help students fulfill their potential" (p. 22).

A concern noted in the *Education Week* article was that the lowest-ranked choice of goals by the school board members was to prepare students for work or college. The larger goal of preparing students to have fulfilling lives trumps the philanthrocapitalism political drive. But, of course, helping students fulfill their potential is very difficult to measure.

INSPIRATION AND HOPE

The ancient Roman philosopher Seneca believed, "It's not because things are difficult that we dare not venture. It's because we dare not venture that they are difficult" (ThinkExist, 1999–2010). To be successful as socially just leaders, what would the characteristics of leadership be? Schooling would be more inclusive, with no extreme disparities. Learning would be more dynamic. Segregation would be a moral wrong, and neighborhoods would be more inclusive.

In this report we have attempted to scaffold the future by addressing what we believe is beyond the status quo. We have discussed the challenges and conjectures from global world crises, the economic end to a single-world-leader country, the technology tools that come at us like a meteor shower impacting the learner daily, while trying to dream of a fairer world where social justice actions are as ubiquitous as technology tools in shaping the lives of students. We therefore offer the *accoutrements* of leadership as necessary transforming attributes required of heroic leaders.

We have written that humans make sense of the future by reflecting on the past. We have used the platform of 2050 and the history of NCPEA to align preparation programs into a meaningful pattern. Mullen (2011) predicts that mid-century public school leadership makes fairness, equality, integrity, and humanity the new standard measure of success.

Martin Luther King Jr. coined the words "nonviolent resister" as necessary for humans to grow and change (Heifetz, 1994). Leadership can be dangerous. We know this, as we live today in a world with 24/7 global news. Generating leadership in our society, Heifetz believes, requires emboldening a greater number of people toward heroic effort: "The long-term challenge of leadership is to develop people's adaptive capacity for tackling an ongoing stream of hard problems" (p. 247).

The curriculum of mid-century is well rounded with a balance of arithmetic, reading, and the arts. The dubious hierarchy of some subjects being treated as better than others has diminished. The arts promote cognition and curiosity and imagination, to name just a few of the characteristics we want to encourage in our students, staff, and leaders.

The mid-century leader realizes that the old ways of thinking from the early twenty-first century are past. Simmons (2010) reminds the mid-century leader to remember that public education, since its inception, has contributed to civic life, strengthened families, valued and contributed to the arts, and respected local cultures and traditions.

Mark Twain once said, "Twenty years from now you will be more disappointed by the things you didn't do than by the ones you did do. So throw off the bowlines. Sail away from the safe harbor. Catch the trade winds in your sails. Explore, Discover" (Khurana, 2011).

Chapter Six

Framing the Preparation of the 2050 Educational Leader

What are the major priorities for preparing educational leaders for their work in school communities? Clues to answering this question are nestled within higher education curricula that are beginning to emerge in many institutions around the nation. They are often pushed by programs that contain thinkers and teachers outside the field of practice, since these are often different eyes that see practice from different dimensions. They have the "outside-in" view instead of the "inside-out" view.

A LEADER PREPARATION EXAMPLE

The curriculum taught to educational leadership students at the University of North Carolina at Greensboro, as an example, was designed to embody the moral vision of faculty members (Mullen, 2010). The courses are anchored in a social justice epistemology expressed as the Statement of Commitments.

This academic covenant resulted from a long process of grappling with how to best convey the professors' passion for preparing students not just to administrate or reform educational communities but also to make such communities socially just. At the master's level, students learn about leadership for teaching and learning, teacher rights and assessment, and the cultural and political dimensions of schooling. At the doctoral level, courses address such issues as race, class, and gender dynamics; ethics and education; and schools as centers of democracy and inquiry.

Technocratic, state-driven priorities for school leaders that highlight finance, management, and testing are not ignored but balanced within a broader curriculum. The faculty members address such organizational content as an integral part of their vision of an equitable education and a just accountability system for schools.

Hence the students are exposed to priorities for exemplary leadership guided by John Dewey's vision of free but disciplined inquiry. The professors see educational work as value laden, and they are transparent about their values of equity and excellence, social justice, and civic activism. Candidates and enrolled students alike write about their priorities for schooling within the context of guiding beliefs. The students' understandings of sociopolitical contexts of education are expanded, and they experience yearlong internships in low-income urban and rural schools.

The professors envision their students as future activists and learning-oriented leaders—some are drawn to these programs, even from abroad, because they are already evolving in this direction. Because moral principles function as the norm in this curriculum, relationships, and decision-making, and because the professors openly hold one another accountable for their beliefs, they feel empowered to make fairness, equity, and excellence cornerstones of their world.

The school leaders they teach struggle with the growing complexity redefining schooling. The faculty members ground the priorities for and standards of schooling in equity and cultural relevance. For example, the students learn that parental involvement, particularly in at-risk schools, is not simply about human resource management; leaders must engage the terrain of school/family relationships and civic deliberation about education, as well as the role of schools, in community transformation.

As morally centered activist-leaders, the students internalize standards for moral reasoning. They are encouraged to develop and make transparent, with their teaching faculties, ethical practices consistent with their collective vision. They grapple with moral dilemmas, such as the individual rights of children and families that combat notions of the common good. As they engage in moral reasoning, they learn to identify and, when possible, minimize or even resolve contradictions that arise in daily work.

Consequently, school leaders can be guided to make sense of culturally relevant issues if they have a social justice orientation. This compass must be rooted in an understanding of the governing principles of accountability and democracy. Leaders are constantly confronted with the opposing priorities of accountability and democracy, but they can empower themselves to discover how these can function as interpenetrating forces.

Social Justice Lenses

Major priorities understood not as principles but as skill sets that guide leadership education in preparing leaders are viewed differently through social justice lenses. Prevalent twenty-first-century priorities that governing standards specify (including innovation, assessment, distributed leadership, and technology, among others) must be vigorously shaped into human rights issues.

Such delineated priorities are otherwise disembodied, lacking an equity focus. They take the reified, traditional form of hierarchical authority, rules and regulations, curricula product adoption, human resources management, and technology efficiency. Technology, for example, can potentially serve as a means for bridging social justice and human services to enhance equity in service to minority and low-income populations, or it can be utilized as an automated strategy for boosting the efficiency and test scores of schools.

High-performing leaders must help teachers prepare students for careers, higher education, citizenship, and global readiness. This is how the national standards in educational leadership read, as well as much of the current literature. But this goal can be either integrated into the kaleidoscope of social justice work or treated in isolation.

Clearly, priorities for leadership must be nurtured within a morally centered social justice framework. For example, future-ready leaders need to know how to innovate by collaborating with partners to facilitate change, remove barriers from learning, and understand global connections. They create a culture that embraces change and make decisions in collaboration with parents and other stakeholders. They also model multiple and authentic assessments to target the skills and knowledge for students. High-quality standardized testing is, at minimum, balanced with alternative assessments that inspire creative student learning.

These leaders enact a diffused leadership strategy that supports teachers' growth through PLCs and positive school climates. They understand leadership activity not as the work of a single leader so much as communal participation. A distributed perspective occurs as principals influence teacher practice as instructional leaders. Cutting-edge technologies not only support teaching and learning but also ensure safety for all, as well as the protection of human dignity.

Priorities for school leadership anchored in a social justice epistemology can enhance administrator advocacy and responsibility. Set adrift of this focus, priorities amplify the inequities and injustices that continue to plague school communities.

Aligning Knowing with Doing

While technological developments abound, empirical research on the effects of e-mentoring and virtual learning is in its infancy (Berry & Marx, 2010), so it is difficult to ascertain the extent to which this platform will promote knowledge about mentoring, learning, motivation, and self-directed learning. Trends and predictions can be hard to separate in trying to envision the future of schools and practitioner preparation programs.

Based on the rising pressure for schools of education to offer distance education and hybrid courses online, with funding clearly focused in that arena, technology adaptations for professors are inevitable. The adjustment may be very gradual for many who are not inclined or do not see connections between their subject and technology; there will continue to be professors who are quick adapters and slow adapters, as well as outright rejectors. But only a few will understand how to move beyond teaching technology and modeling efficient uses of technology for active learning in the fourth mode.

Faculty members in educational leadership and teacher education will be challenged to model the integration of social learning technologies, probably with greater persistence over the next five years, let alone the next thirty years. Education schools will strive for relevance by modeling twenty-first-century technologies, but it is the fourth mode that is an unknown.

Technology will not be relegated to a peripheral academic reference or passive blackboard repository. Attention on technology learning and integration should prove to be a major source of attention for educator and leader preparation for impoverished schools, Title I schools, and low-performing schools. Emphases still needed will focus on the connection between technology and learning, learner-centered leading, changing classrooms and schools that are not conducive to twenty-first-century learning, the concept and practice of work-arounds, and educational coaching for new teachers and leaders.

The Future Is On the Horizon and Here

University preparation programs have been moving toward new standards of performance and experience within accepted academic frameworks (Berry & Williamson, 2009) that could potentially promote "a better balance between the science and art of leading" (English, 2008, p. ix). This changing curriculum has been described using such language as *problem-based, experiential, constructivist, ethnic-oriented*, and certainly *student-centered*, which suggests that the pedagogy taught in university-based programs will need to move learning to center stage and the responsibility for learning more to the learner.

Learners represent a continuum of constituents from the prospective leader (university student) to the teacher and, most importantly, the child or adolescent in the classroom. Such initiatives as high-quality, yearlong internships for prospective leaders may be essential to merging the applied nature of the profession with the academic nature of the discipline. When we adopt aesthetics as a language of possibility for mid-century leadership, students learn through art and aesthetics (not just science and empiricism) to foster a democratic society and a highly engaged global citizenry (English, 2008, 2011a).

We need to balance the rational, theoretical, and scientific emphasis in preparation programs with emotional, applied, and artistic domains of knowing (English, 2008, 2011a). The problem-based, experiential, performance approach extends, refines, and reconnects the applied educational leadership curriculum to the academic curriculum that arose in the 1950s (Berry & Williamson, 2009).

The applied nature of the field is being reinforced by standards that have performance expectations and requirements. To imbue the educational leadership curriculum with meaningful performance activities that replicate day-to-day experience is an attempt to reconnect the professional and theory-based aspects of educational administration to its more practical and applied elements of leading and managing educational organizations.

The adaptation of performance and experiential learning as dimensions of the aesthetic in educational preparation is returning to the very practical knowledge of *what to do* and *how to do it*. It is becoming clear that professors are recognizing the importance of merging applied knowledge with practical knowing and theoretical constructs within educational leadership preparation.

Faculty members are teaching students and learning from students, and they are teaching each other to attain higher levels of technology integration and learning. They are pushing the envelope on learning through podcasts, video streaming, online chats, and assessments following course completion.

We, the authors, use such technologies in our own leading, teaching, and communications, in addition to Elluminate, blogs, Skype, iPhones, and more. Digital portfolios will be common (Lackney, 2011). However, some classroom teachers who are given innovative technologies, including digital portfolio tools and programs, simply do not use them (Peck et al., 2011), which implies that wasted opportunities and resources must be constructively addressed by leaders.

Educational leadership programs are providing leadership in such ways as incorporating e-portfolios as a significant formative and summative assessment tool and as a method for better engaging students' creativity. Putting personalized technology artifacts in place for assessing student learning is one of the best indicators we seem to have at this time of accountability and our commitment to it (Berry & Williamson, 2009).

In the learning in technology era, leaders will face the challenge not only of navigating technology reform but also of developing strategies for engaging youth in digital media culture (Peck et al., 2011). While these two challenges are already evident in some schools, they will intensify in the future and reflect opportunities for growth and success.

Based on the few available studies of evidence-based practice in high schools, school leaders are encountering more specific technology-related challenges—namely, troublesome support structures that negatively affect technology implementation, a taxing obligation to encourage and police student technology use, and a digital media culture through which students contest authority, power, and other established structures (e.g., Peck et al., 2011).

Responding to challenges like these, school leaders are using work-arounds to alleviate technology problems and adopting innovative, technology-friendly instructional practices. Professors in educational leadership programs will find that their students who are currently teachers and assistant principals, as well as curriculum and technology leaders, deal with these major challenges in their daily work.

Importantly, educational, mentoring, and coaching interventions through teacher-guided pedagogy and instruction will need much more attention in schools (Dickey, 2011; Fletcher & Mullen, in press) and educational leadership programs (Peck et al., 2011). Dickey's case study of inservice teachers' hands-on exploration within multiuser virtual environments is vital for revealing how practicing teachers themselves might be responding to the game-based learning environments that many students are immersed in these days.

Based on a workshop experience in a graduate course from 2007 to 2008, eight K–12 teachers experienced their first interactive intervention through which they documented their own learning and concerns. Teacher discovery was promoted through guided instructional uses of several software applications (i.e., Second Life and Active Worlds Educational Universe). Results indicated that the teacher sample saw the educational potential for new kinds of pedagogical engagement through "learning by doing" for their own students. These inservice teachers expressed delight in creating their own avatars and building virtual worlds that they themselves attempted to link to their specific content areas. One of the teachers liked how she could "swing [her] line of vision," although the other side of this benefit was that she also experienced unusual sensations, such as nausea, not unlike being on a roller coaster (Dickey, 2011, p. 8).

To summarize, some educational strengths that emerged out of multimedia programs through which virtual worlds are a facilitated phenomenon are as follows:

- Some flexibility for customizing objects and creating images of one's own, which could offer K–12 students constructivist and creative advantages for learning
- Artistic benefits, including the creation of visual representations, control over movements that extend to objects and avatars, and the building of new worlds (e.g., potentially castles, villages) using a library of objects
- Ease of personal interactivity facilitating group interaction and shared interactivity with designated others and groups
- Software features that allow adults to focus on contact and become immersed in personal expression (Dickey, 2011)

Drawbacks of the same software are listed below:

- High learning curve, requiring time to navigate multimedia environments (e.g., building objects) before being able to engage in relevant learning
- Overwhelming time investment in learning, creating, and teaching

- Objectionable content in multimedia software that is too mature for youth and younger audiences, including pornography and gender stereotypes of perfection (typically built into avatars with idealized shapes)
- Issues of safety, security, and control over contact through avatar interactions and outside influences, all currently not within the purview of teachers (Dickey, 2011)

Importantly, the teachers who kept reflective journals offered experientially attuned critiques that, if further developed, could produce effective, targeted learning for students.

The theory and pragmatics of virtual worlds for educational leadership programs could be introduced as part of such larger initiatives as learning community development for teachers and students and grassroots comprehensive staff development. As a related point, understanding human development, reciprocity, and the relational skills that foster mutual learning and coleading are essential.

Successful teamwork and problem solving are added elements for close consideration, as they hinge on the capacity for adults to function as interactively guided, self-directed active learners (Mullen, 2009; Papa, 2011a). Reciprocity understood more fully and deeply as a teaching-learning relationship with and among educators and students, as opposed to technically and hierarchically, disfavors the notion that one acts on another to achieve ends.

Philosopher Martin Buber (1970) referred to this as "universal reciprocity," situating the leader and learner "in service in the universe" (p. 67). This idea opens up the possibility that acts of helping, healing, educating, raising, and redeeming belong to all and that children are educators as well.

On the surface, as a contradiction to this whole-school relational idea, real-time assessments are coming into vogue and will become the norm, probably even for the more open-ended tasks for which assessment designs may be under way. The attraction is that student work will be scored more easily and quickly using time-saving devices. "Grading" is shifting to on-demand electronic scoring assessments through secure Internet connections (Johnson, Penny, & Gordon, 2008). This will minimize teacher time, based on teacher demand.

Mid-century leaders, like their predecessors of today and tomorrow, will recognize the need for teachers to spend time in communities. But it is the mid-century leader who will likely figure out work-arounds for how these may occur less out of the classroom and more through teachers' work during class time with technology adaptations, feedback loops, communities inside and outside buildings, global networks, and virtual communities. Technology immersion training as connected with student assessment will require focus within learning communities and schools of the future.

Finally, in this chapter we have conceived of the mid-century leader as a digitally attuned humanitarian who is well equipped to contend with the challenges of tomorrow's schools. We believe that university-based preparation programs have a serious and vital role to play in preparing tomorrow's teachers, principals, superintendents, and other leaders, and that much of this preparation needs to focus on learning in technology as a new cultural standard of excellence and equity for schooling environments.

Chapter Seven

Re-centering Our Field

Pedagogically Centered Leadership

This chapter presents our most radical, but (we believe) very possible, idea of re-centering our field by 2050. In most schools or colleges of education, educational leadership and/or administration is a separate department or program. There are historic reasons for such structured silos.

The first is the evolution of administrative roles away from that of classroom teacher in which business functions became dominant over instructional ones (Callahan, 1962; Glass, 2004). The second is the outright discriminatory practices based on gender bias in early programs to prepare school administrators, including setting "low quotas on the number of women who could enroll, some allowing no more than 2 percent of available slots to go to women" (Blount, 1998, p. 118).

Teacher education has been dominated by females because teaching was historically considered "women's work" (Ortiz & Marshall, 1988, p. 123). Those who established educational administration programs and who became dominant in them were determined not to let their ranks become "overfeminized," because the

presence of too many women meant the loss of status in the educational occupational hierarchy that was developing at the time
(Shakeshaft, 2011).

The emerging subject matter of educational administration was
also considered decidedly androcentric and either took a hostile
stance toward women or emphasized matters of "organizational
structure" over interpersonal and instructionally centered views
(Shakeshaft, 1993, p. 100).

These historic perspectives and biases have led to preparation
programs that, while "about" instructional leadership, really have
very little to do with the essence of schooling: learning and teaching. The "theory movement" in educational administration also
pushed the field into positioning matters of structure and management at the forefront, thus marginalizing where the actual process
of education occurred.

Where we should go is what Gunter observed almost a decade
ago:

> What we need is less emphasis on restructuring hierarchical
> leadership and more courage to enable teachers and students
> with managers to work on developing learning processes and the
> contextual settings in which they are located. Such an approach
> would politicise schools around pedagogy rather than around
> glossy manifestos, and it would also mean that the relationship
> between schools and HEI's [higher education institutions] might
> be based more on knowledge creation than on current imposed
> trends towards contractualism. (2002, p. 138)

Similarly, our task force believes it is time to integrate programs
and departments of educational leadership/administration with
teacher preparation programs, and in this perspective we are not
alone. We note that in 2008, in a national study of educational
leadership programs in six states comprising fifty-four preparation

programs, Murphy, Moorman, and McCarthy (2008) documented many failures of preparation programs to be responsive to new requirements.

One of this team's recommendations was that the culture of autonomy regnant in schools of education be replaced with a culture of community. They noted, "Historically, we have neither desired nor required much collaboration and integration. Individualism, autonomy, and separation reign supreme" (p. 8). Building a *culture of community* not only makes sense within a school of education, but it also makes sense for the kind of leadership schools will require by mid-century.

PEDAGOGICALLY CENTERED LEADERSHIP

Education is about learning first, teaching second, and then everything else in support of those functions. Management is required to support the learning and teaching process. In too many of our programs to prepare educational leaders, they are trained as though it didn't matter what the function is. It could be assembly-line washing machines or fourth-grade language arts.

Management is a "generalism." When it doesn't matter what the function is for leadership or management, then any program to prepare them will do. We can hardly complain when our preparation programs are generic that any sort of special licensing or consideration is required at all. Another consequence of that approach is that we end up with retired army generals who know little to nothing about the purpose or function of civic education centered on learning and teaching in a democracy running school systems.

We reject business models as appropriate for educational leadership because they have little or nothing to do with the purpose of education and say very little about matters of pedagogy, curriculum, or learning, the central work of schools. Business models are anchored in economics that require prediction and control. Corporate models are lodged in top-down, authoritarian approaches to management. The idea that business schools could prepare management professionals or make management a profession has been a documented failure (Khurana, 2007).

A host of new deans of business schools have publicly indicated they need to change the dominant "win-at-all-costs culture" (Middleton, 2010a). The new dean of the Harvard Business School admitted, "I believe that management education has been overly focused on the principles of management" (Middleton, 2010b). We could issue a similar criticism of educational administration programs.

We believe that future schools must include teachers as leaders, that schools must become more democratic and collegial places with diffused pedagogical practices, and that the "win-at-all-costs" *viz* test score obsession must be replaced with more healthful, humane, and balanced educational programming. But most important for programs preparing educational leaders, the purpose of schools is not to improve their management, but to improve the learning in them. There has been a mistaken picture of the role of management. Poorly performing schools are usually places where not much learning is going on, and they lack obvious good management to produce order and discipline. So the antidote looks simple: install better management. But there are plenty of schools managed reasonably well where learning is still not very good (Papa & English, 2011). Better management does not produce better learning, unless what comprises "better management" includes those practices that lead to improved learning beyond what measured by standardized tests.

Leadership models have to be constructed to place learning and teaching at the center instead of the margins. While social science approaches have helped construct some useful ideas of important structures, they have largely ignored the fundamental functions of schooling. Emphasizing climate and culture, while important, makes little difference about learning if they are not defined by learning.

The major issue here is that school administration was never designed around the principles of learning or teaching. It was designed to provide order and discipline into which a model of teaching and learning was placed. The nub of the conceptual, philosophical, and attitudinal approach to administration and leadership has been that in the preparation of leaders, we have grounded them not in principles of learning and teaching, but in models of managerial efficiency, order, and organizational harmony.

Models of schooling effectiveness reflect order first, learning second. And while common sense would dictate that without order there can be no learning, there is abundant evidence that learning takes place in every condition known to humanity. The relationship between chaos and creativity is also known.

THE EARMARKS OF PEDAGOGICALLY CENTERED LEADERSHIP

Here are the organizing centers for a pedagogically centered leadership (derived from Hollins, 2011, p. 397):

1. knowledge of how humans grow and develop, which includes group-based development and cultural differences in the home and family, which then "inform the design of learning experiences and the specific ways in which learning is facilitated" (p. 397);
2. an intensive understanding about the learning process itself and how that understanding can be employed to enhance learning;

3. an extensive knowledge of discipline and domain-specific conceptual patterns and how they inform the discourse in those disciplines;

4. an understanding of how specific pedagogical practices are related to specific theoretical perspectives and how they are focused by and on a specific philosophical position to attain immediate and longer-term learning outcomes;

5. the use of a variety of assessment strategies to evaluate pedagogical practices, which includes the use of authentic assessment models; and

6. how to connect and integrate all of the above to the creation of the common core curriculum standards currently being developed.

Finally, Hollins's essential knowledges contain a capstone description of what we believe is the essence of pedagogically centered leadership, which includes principals and teachers working with a collegial and less structured and hierarchical context:

> An ability to maintain a strong professional identity, engage in self-directed professional growth and development, recognize characteristics and qualities of professional communities in different contexts, and work collaboratively with colleagues within a professional community to improve learning outcomes. (2011, p. 397)

WHY THIS LEADERSHIP APPROACH?

We view the concept of pedagogically centered leadership in the schools, and with it the conjunction of preparation programs in the university involving educational administration and leadership and teacher preparation, as a joining of the development of all profes-

sionals who work in the schools. York-Barr and Duke (2004) indicate that there are three reasons teacher leadership has been offered
as an antidote to ineffective schools.

The first is that teacher involvement leads to improved commitment and taking ownership of the school's goals. The drawback of
this approach is that such involvement is too often proffered by the
principal and that it remains the province of the principal as to
"whether" teachers are "involved" or not. The clear distinction between administrative and teaching roles remains, and the hierarchy
that defines superior/subordinate roles is merely "softened" or "hu-
manized."

The second notion of teacher leadership is that teachers possess
unique forms of craft knowledge based on best practices and that
the school organization should be such that such knowledge is
shared and advanced. A third rationale for teacher leadership is that
by uplifting teaching as a career, it will be possible to form career
patterns of advancement that will retain the most talented practitioners in the classroom or in closely related proximity.

We see a pedagogically centered leadership as collegial, participatory, and democratic in nature and, in that sense, one that de-
centers hierarchy and blurs or bends superior/subordinate relationships, creating new combinations of relationships that are more
contextually sensitive to the work to be accomplished. We see such
ideas as *parallel leadership* (Crowther, Kaagan, Ferguson, & Hann,
2002) or *distributed leadership* (Spillane, Halverson, & Diamond,
2001), in which tasks are spread out among many participants as
approaching a new nucleus of community, but we envision even
something more integrated than either of these ideas.

Pedagogically centered leadership is more than a recognition of
the outstanding traditional, highly technical competent classroom
practitioner. While technical competence in the process of teaching
is certainly an expected prerequisite, there have to be included in
formal preparation things that often appear in the curricula of edu-

cational leadership programs, such as "theories of leadership, human resource development, organizational learning and development, work design, and power" (York-Barr & Duke, 2004, p. 291).

We also see combining the fields of educational leadership and teacher leadership as providing the basis for more democratically operated schools and, as noted by Woods, "the dispersal of leadership that embraces teachers can encompass aims that promote democracy and social justice" (2005, p. 62). The connection between a more democratic pedagogy and the pursuit of social justice go hand in hand. We therefore see these developments as offering a powerful re-centering of educational leadership for mid-century public education.

ANTICIPATING THE PUSHBACK

One has to fight for good ideas to become practice. We see the following sources of resistance to re-centering our field:

1. *Current Educational Accreditation Standards*—Current national standards used for accreditation of educational leadership programs and departments embody the solitary heroic leader model, thoroughly at the top of the hierarchical management pyramid, which is found almost everywhere at century's beginning. While the standards often talk about "collaborative leadership," it is never truly democratic in any sense, and it is centered on dominant organizational and business models that are not pedagogically grounded. Such standards would have to be changed.

2. *Mindsets and Measurement Modalities*—Many people in schools contribute to pupil learning. The diffusion of responsibility for teaching and, hence, learning will muddy the waters surrounding notions of accountability, especially when it comes to pay-for-performance plans that are grounded on the

idea that individuals can be held solely responsible for given quantities of learning. Current "line/staff" management models make such plans appear feasible, despite recent research that shows merit pay has no influence on pupil achievement (Springer et al., 2010).

3. *Current Silos in Schools of Education*—There are many barriers internal to schools of education that will be present to push back on the notion of pedagogically centered leadership. Both fields will require re-centering teacher educators away from an exclusive focus on technical classroom-centered mastery to include additional work on the sociology of schools as holistic entities and knowledge of working with adults as well as children. Educational administration texts and courses will have to include more theoretical perspectives on the art and science of teaching, curriculum theory and development, and working with teachers as colleagues.

While the idea of distributive leadership is popular in some quarters, it is only a midpoint in the continuum toward a truly collaborative work environment of schools at mid-century.

THE PROMISE OF MID-CENTURY CHANGE

The merging of educational leadership and teacher education into a pedagogically centered focus holds great promise to restore to schools a more humane outlook regarding the function of education. School leadership is not first and foremost about test scores, but rather about enabling children to become more fully human with a recognition of their inherent worth and a valuing of their capabilities in all fields, not merely math and science.

We believe that such a restoration will foster a more democratic work environment and lead to practical strategies to approach the many social inequalities that continue to lock millions of children and their families into permanent and perpetuating second-class citizenship.

Epilogue

Tempus Fugit!

We have argued in this book for an educational leadership in 2050 that is unlike the one we have today. Across a very broad front of external challenges and internal consolidations, we see a field, if not in retreat, then in stasis. The once dominant outlook on the meaning of public school leadership as rooted in the ethic of service and civic humanism that animated our field is under a full-scale assault from market-centered ideologies rooted in the profit motive advanced by the dictates of federal and state government policies and the top-down agendas of the billion-dollar foundations pushing their business-centered agendas.

With this push, we see the return of school racial segregation and isolation, and despite millions of dollars being invested in business solutions imposed on school systems, we see no discernible improvement in impacting the achievement gap, nor any that would broach the ever-widening wealth differential between the social "haves" and "have-nots" in the United States.

The schools do not function in a vacuum. They represent somebody's values, and those have been (and continue to be) the social classes that see in them the means to retain their social and political power. That schools should benefit a greater proportion of all children means recognizing why they do not do so now. From that analysis, we believe that means we must take up the cause of social justice not only in schools but in our larger society as well.

We believe that the time is ripe for a re-centering of our field and reorganizing leadership practice around issues of pedagogy, teaching, and learning as opposed to those of management. The isolation of educational leadership departments and programs have accentuated the "generic managerialism" of the neoliberal assault on our programs, which argues that business management techniques are superior to those found in educational leadership programs in schools of education and that it makes no difference where leaders are prepared, since we simply need to find those most genetically disposed toward "greatness."

We pose a different vision and a different future for 2050. There is nothing utopian about our advocacy. We think there are many ways to arrive at this different notion of school leadership, and while 2050 may seem like a long way off, it will arrive as quickly as the passage of the last forty years.

The sobering insight is that if we do not actively work to reshape our field, it will arrive having been shaped by others. In that case, we will become the means to somebody else's ends. We have serious reservations about the ends being advanced by others, as we have delineated in this special report. This is not the time to stand on the sidelines and be objective observers. These are the times in which the voices of the profession, scholars and practitioners, must be heard. We hope this report helps to raise those voices to embrace renewed hope and optimism in our democracy and the cause of social justice in the larger social fabric of the nation.

References

Aarons, D. (2010, September 22). Rhee reflective in aftershock of D.C. primary. *Education Week, 30*(4), 1, 17.

Adams, R., & Vascellaro, J. (2010, December 13). News Corp. draws study plan. *Wall Street Journal.*

Anderson, G., & Herr, K. (2011, August/September). Scaling up "evidence-based" practices for teachers is a profitable but discredited paradigm. *Educational Rsearcher, 40*(6), 287–89.

Anderson, G., & Pini, M. (2011). Educational leadership in the new economy: Keeping the "public" in public schools. In F. English (Ed.), *The SAGE Handbook of Educational Leadership* (2nd ed., pp. 176–94). Thousand Oaks, CA: Sage.

Anderson, L. (2011, May–June). Demystifying the Arab Spring. *Foreign Affairs, 90*(3), 2–6.

Anonymous (2011, July 15). The fear and frustration of faculty at for-profit colleges. *Chronicle of Higher Education,* B12–13.

Apple, M. (2011). Global crises, social justice, and teacher education. *Journal of Teacher Education, 62*(2), 222–34.

Archbald, D. (2008, December). Research versus problem solving for the education leadership doctoral thesis: Implications for form and function. *Educational Administration Quarterly, 44*(5), 704–39.

Baker, B., Orr, M., & Young, M. (2007, August). Academic drift, institutional production, and professional distribution of graduate dgrees in educational leadership. *Educational Administration Quarterly, 43*(3), 279–318.

Banchero, S. (2010, July 24–25). Teachers lose jobs over test scores. *Wall Street Journal,* A3.

Barnett, J. H., & Archambault, L. (2010). The gaming effect: How massive multi-player online games incorporate principles of economics. *Tech Trends, 54*(6), 29–35. Retrieved March 11, 2011, from http://cnx.org/content/col11122/1.1.

Barry, B. (2005). *Why social justice matters.* Cambridge: Polity Press.

Bartlett, J. (1968). *Familiar quotations* (14th ed.). Boston: Little, Brown.

Berry, J. E., & Marx, G. (2010). Adapting to the pedagogy of technology in educational administration. *Scholar–Practitioner Quarterly, 4*, 245–55.

Berry, J. E., & Williamson, R. (Eds.). (2009). *Performance assessment in educational leadership programs.* Rice University, Houston, TX: Connexions. Retrieved March 11, 2011, from http://cnx.org/content/col11122/1.1.

Betts, R. (2010, November/December). Conflict or cooperation? Three visions revisited. *Foreign Affairs, 89*(6), 186–94.

Birdsall, N., & Fukuyama, F. (2011, March–April). The post-Washington consensus: Development after the crisis. *Foreign Affairs, 90*(2), 45–53.

Blount, J. (1998). *Destined to rule the schools: Women and the superintendency, 1873–1995.* Albany: State University of New York Press.

Blumenstyk, G. (2004, May 14). For-profit colleges face new scrutiny. *Chronicle of Higher Education*, A1–29.

Blumenstyk, G., & Richards, A. (2011, March 18). For-profit colleges manage defaults to mask problems, analysis indicates. *Chronicle of Higher Education*, A1, A6–7.

Bourdieu, P. (1999). The abdication of the state. In P. Bourdieu et al. (Eds.), *The weight of the world: Social suffering in contemporary society* (pp. 181–88). Stanford, CA: Stanford University Press.

Bourdieu, P. (1998). *Acts of resistance: Against the tyranny of the market.* New York: New Press.

Bourdieu, P. (1993). *The field of cultural production.* New York: Columbia University Press.

Bourdieu, P. (1985). The social space and the genesis of groups. *Theory and Society, 14*, 723–44.

Bourdieu, P., & Passeron, J-C. (2000). *Reproduction in education, society and culture* (2nd ed.). Thousand Oaks, CA: Sage.

Bourdieu, P., & Passeron, J-C. (1979). *The inheritors: French students and their relation to culture.* Chicago: University of Chicago Press.

Bowles, S., Gintis, H., & Groves, M. (2005). *Unequal chances: Family background and economic success.* New York: Russell Sage Foundation.

Brantlinger, E. (2003). *Dividing classes: How the middle class school negotiates and rationalizes school advantage.* New York: Routledge Falmer.

Briefing America and China: By fits and starts (2010, February 6). *Economist, 394*(8668), 25.

Broad Foundation & Thomas B. Fordham Institute (2003). *Better leaders for America's schools: A manifesto.* Retrieved from www.edexcellencemedia.net/publications/2003/200305_betterleaders/manifesto.pdf.

Brown, J. S. (2000). Growing up digital: How the Web changes work, education, and the ways people learn. *Change*, 10–20. Retrieved March 10, 2011, from www.johnseelybrown.com/Growing_up_digital.pdf.

Buber, M. (1970). *I and thou.* New York: Simon & Schuster.

Butts, R. (1999). Testability. In R. Audi (Ed.), *The Cambridge dictionary of philosophy* (2nd ed.). Cambridge: Cambridge University Press.

Callahan, R. (1962). *Education and the cult of efficiency.* Chicago: University of Chicago Press.

Campbell, R. F., & Newell, L. J. (1973). *A study of professors of educational administration.* Columbus, OH: University Council For Educational Administration.

Carnes, M. C. (2011, March 11). Setting students' minds on fire. *Chronicle of Higher Education, 57*(27), A72.

Cary, K. (2010, July 30). Why do you think they're called for-profit colleges? *Chronicle of Higher Education,* A88.

Cassidy, J. (2009). *How markets fail: The logic of economic calamities.* New York: Farrar, Straus & Giroux.

Chamberlain, L. M., & Kindred, L. W. (1949). *The teacher and school organization* (2nd ed.). New York: Prentice Hall.

Christensen, C. M., Horn, M. B., Caldera, L., & Soares, L. (2011, February). *Disrupting college: How disruptive innovation can deliver quality and affordability to postsecondary education* (pp. 1–72). Retrieved March 11, 2011, from www.americanprogress.org/issues/2011/02/pdf/disrupting_college.pdf.

Christensen, C., Horn, M. B., & Johnson, C. W. (2008). *Disrupting class: How disruptive innovation will change the way the world learns.* New York: McGraw-Hill.

Christensen, T. (2011, March/April). The advantages of an assertive China. *Foreign Affairs, 90*(2), 54–67.

Collins, J. W., III, & O'Brien, N. P. (2003). Imagination. In J. W. Collins III and N. P. O'Brien (Eds.), *The Greenwood dictionary of education.* Westport, CT: Greenwood Press.

Collins, R. (1998). *The sociology of philosophies: A global theory of intellectual change.* Cambridge, MA: Harvard University Press.

Condron, D. J. (2011). Egalitarianism and educational excellence: Compatible goals for affluent societies. *Educational Researcher, 40*(2), 47–55.

Creighton, T. (2011). Entrepreneurial leadership for teaching. In R. Papa (Ed.), *Technology leadership for school improvement* (pp. 3–20). Thousand Oaks, CA: Sage.

Creighton, T. (2005). *Leading from below the surface: A non-traditional approach to school leadership.* Thousand Oaks, CA: Corwin.

Crowther, F., Kaagan, S., Ferguson, M., & Hann, L. (2002). *Developing teacher leaders: How teacher leadership enhances school success.* Thousand Oaks, CA: Corwin.

Davis, S., Davis, D., & Williams, D. (2010). Challenges and issues facing the future of nursing education: Implications for ethnic minority faculty and students. *Journal of Cultural Diversity, 17*(4), 122–26.

Dickey, M. D. (2011). The pragmatics of virtual works for K–12 educators: Investigating the affordances and constraints of *Active Worlds* and *Second Life* with K–12 in-service teachers. *Educational Technology Research & Development, 59*(1), 1–20.

Dictionary.com. (2011). s.v. prognosticating. Retrieved March 6, 2011, from http://dictionary.reference.com/browse/prognosticating.

Dougherty, C. (2011, September 14). How to accurately measure the poor remains elusive. *Wall Street Journal*, A4.

Economics focus: Don't look down. *Economist* (2011, August 13), 74.

Eisner, E. W. (2005). *Reimagining schools: The selected works of Elliot W. Eisner*. London: Routledge.

Engelhardt, F. (1931). *Public school organization and administration*. Boston: Ginn.

English, F. (2011a). Educational leadership at century's beginning: A continuing search for the philosopher's stone. Introduction in F. English (Ed.), *The Sage handbook of educational leadership: Advances in theory, research, and practice* (2nd ed., pp.vii–xiii). Thousand Oaks, CA: Sage.

English, F. (2011b). *Caveat emptor: Buyer beware of some inter-agency and non-profit collaboration with neoliberal foundations and think tanks*. Paper presented at the National Council of Professors of Educational Administration Summer Conference, Portland, Oregon.

English, F. (2009). Editors' introduction: Best of the best: The most influential international writing in educational administration in the last forty years. In F. English, J. G. Lumby, R. Papa, E. A. Samier, & A. D. Walker (Eds.), *Educational leadership & administration, vol. 1–4*. Los Angeles: Sage.

English, F. W. (2008). *The art of educational leadership: Balancing performance and accountability*. Thousand Oaks, CA: Sage.

English, F. (2007). The NRC's *Scientific Research in Education*: It isn't even wrong. In F. English and G. Furman (Eds.), *Research and educational leadership: Navigating the new National Research Council guidelines* (pp. 1–38). Lanham, MD: Rowman & Littlefield Education.

English, F. (2006, August). The unintended consequences of a standardized knowledge base in advancing educational leadership preparation. *Educational Administration Quarterly, 42*(3), 461–72.

English, F. (2004). Learning "Manifestospeak": A metadiscursive analysis of the Fordham Institute's and Broad Foundation's Manifesto for Better Leaders for America's Schools. In T. Lasley (Ed.), *Better leaders for America's schools: Perspectives on the Manifesto* (pp. 52–91). Columbia, MO: University Council for Educational Administration.

English, F. (2003, March). Cookie-cutter leaders for cookie-cutter schools: The teleology of standardization and the de-legitimization of the university in educational leadership preparation. *Leadership and Policy in Schools, 2*(1), 27–46.

English, F. (2002, March). The point of scientificity, the fall of the epistemological dominos, and the end of the field of educational administration. *Studies in Philosophy and Education, 2*(2) 109–36.

English, F., & Papa, R. (2010). *Restoring human agency to educational administration: Status and strategies.* Lancaster, PA: ProActive.

Erdahl, R. (2010). As cited in P. Woods (2011). *Transforming education policy: Shaping a democratic future.* Bristol: Polity Press

Farrall, L. (2011, March/April). How al Qaeda works. *Foreign Affairs, 90*(2), 128–39.

Field, K. (2011, May 13). Faculty at for-profits allege constant pressure to keep students enrolled. *Chronicle of Higher Education,* A1–10.

Flesher W. R., & Knoblauch, A. (1957). *A decade of development in educational leadership.* National Conference of Professors of Educational Administration.

Fletcher, S., & Mullen, C. A. (Eds.). (in press). *The SAGE handbook of mentoring and coaching in education.* Thousand Oaks, CA: Sage.

For-profit colleges: Monsters in the making? (2010, July 24). *Economist,* 36.

Foucault, M. (1972). *The archaeology of knowledge.* New York: Pantheon.

Fox, J. (2009). *The myth of the rational market: A history of risk, reward, and delusion on Wall Street.* New York: HarperCollins.

Fox, L. (2003). *Enron: The rise and fall.* Hoboken, NJ: Wiley.

Fraser, N. (2007). Re-framing justice in a globalizing world. In T. Lovell (Ed.), *(Mis)recognition, social inequality and social justice: Nancy Fraser and Pierre Bourdieu* (pp. 17–35). New York: Routledge.

Fusarelli, L. (2004, January 14). The new consumerism in educational leadership. *Education Week, 23*(18), 28.

Gillum, J., & Bello, M. (2011, April 17). When standardized test scores soared in D.C., were the gains real? *USA Today.* Retrieved March 28, 2011, from http://www.usatoday.com/news/education.

Glaser, C. (2011, March/April). Will China's rise lead to war? *Foreign Affairs, 90*(2), 80–91.

Glass, T. (2004). *The history of educational administration viewed through its textbooks.* Lanham, MD: Scarecrow Press.

Global progress report, 2010. (2010, January). *Current History, 109*(723), 3.

Golden, O., Macomber, J., & Harwood, R. (2008). *Commentary on children, metro trends: Mismatch between local resources today and investment needs for the nation's future.* Retrieved March 6, 2011, from www.metrotrends.org/commentary/children.cfm.

Goldman, D. (2009). *Great recession vs. great depression: CNNMoney.com.* Retrieved March 12, 2011, from http://money.cnn.com/news/storysupplement/economy/recession_depression.

Goodwin, B., & Ristvey, J. (2011, April). Putting a little mystery in teaching: Teachers can tap students' natural curiosity to generate interesting lessons. *Principal Leadership*, 24–27.

Grading the moneymen. (May 1, 2011). *Newsweek.* Retrieved from www.newsweek.com/2011/05/01 grading-the-moneymen.html.

Grady, M. L. (2011). *Leading the technology-powered school.* Thousand Oaks, CA: Corwin.

Grenfell, M. (2007). *Pierre Bourdieu: Education and training.* London: Continuum.

Griffiths, D. E., Stout, R. T., & Forsyth, P. B. (1988). *Leaders for America's schools: The report and papers of the National Commission on Excellence in Educational Administration.* Berkeley, CA: McCutchan Publishing.

Gunter, H. (2002). *Leaders and leadership in education.* London: Paul Chapman.

Hackmann, D. G., & McCarthy, M. M. (2011). *At a crossroads: The educational leadership professoriate in the 21st century.* Charlotte, NC: Information Age Publishing.

Halbfinger, D. (2011, April 8). An ever-growing image of a stumbling third term. *New York Times*, A20.

Hanushek, E. (2010, October 19). There is no "war on teachers." *Wall Street Journal*, A17.

Heifetz, R. A. (1994). *Leadership without easy answers.* Cambridge, MA: Belknap.

Heilbrunn, J. (1996). Can leadership be studied? In P. Temes (Ed.), *Teaching leadership: Essays in theory and practice* (pp. 1–13). New York: Peter Lang.

Helliker, K. (2011, August 29). Public more skeptical of online college courses. *Wall Street Journal*, A8.

Henze, R., & Arriaza, G. (2006). Language and reforming schools: A case for a critical approach to language in educational leadership. *International Journal of Leadership in Education, 9*(2), 157–77.

Hernstein, R., & Murray, C. (2004). *The bell curve.* New York: Free Press.

Hess, F. (2004). A license to lead? In T. Lasley (Ed.), *Better leaders for America's schools: Perspective on the Manifesto* (UCEA Monograph, pp. 35–51). Columbia, MO: UCEA.

Hess, F. (2003). *A license to lead? A new leadership agenda for America's schools.* Washington, DC: Progressive Policy Institute.

Hollins, E. (2011, September/October). Teacher preparation for quality teaching. *Journal of Teacher Education, 62*(4), 395–407.

Irvin, G. (2008). *Super rich: The rise of inequality in Britain and the United States.* Cambridge: Polity Press.

Jensen, E. (2009). *Teaching with poverty in mind: What being poor does to kids' brains and what schools can do about it.* Retrieved April 2, 2011, from www.ascd.org/publications/books/109074/chapters/Understanding-the-Nature-of-Poverty.aspx.

Jisi, W. (2011, March/April). China's search for a grand strategy. *Foreign Affairs, 90*(2), 80–91.

Johnson, H. B. (2006). *The American dream and the power of wealth: Choosing schools and inheriting inequality in the land of opportunity.* New York: Routledge.

Johnson, R. L., Penny, J. A., & Gordon, B. (2008). *Assessing performance: Designing, scoring, and validating performance tasks.* New York: Guilford.

Jolliffe, D. (2004). *Rural poverty at a glance.* Rural Development Research Report, RDRR No. 100. Washington, DC: USDA Economic Research Service. Available March 27, 2007, at www.ers.usda.gov/publications/rdrr100/rdrr100.pdf.

Josephson, M. (2002). *Making ethical decisions.* Marina Del Ray, CA: Josephson Institute of Ethics.

Kaufman, R., Herman, J., & Watters, K. (1996). *Educational planning: Strategic, tactical, operational.* Lancaster, PA: Technomic.

Keegan, J. (1987). *The mask of command.* New York: Viking.

Khurana, R. (2007). *From higher aims to hired hands: The social transformation of American business schools and the unfulfilled promise of management as a profession.* Princeton, NJ: Princeton University Press.

Khurana, R. (2002). *Searching for a corporate savior: The irrational quest for charismatic CEOs.* Princeton, NJ: Princeton University Press.

Khurana, S. (2011). *Mark Twain quotes: About.com guide.* Retrieved April 9, 2011, from http://quotations.about.com/od/stillmorefamouspeople/a/Mark Twain2.htm.

Kimber, M., & Ehrich, L. (2011). The democratic deficit and school-based management in Australia. *Journal of Educational Administration, 49*(2), 179–99.

Klein, J. (2011, August 20–21). Learning the hard way. *Wall Street Journal*, C1.

Klein, J. (2010, December 4–5). What I learned at the education barricades. *Wall Street Journal*, A13.

Lackney, J. A. (2011). New approaches for school design. In F. W. English (Ed.), *The Sage handbook of educational leadership* (2nd ed., pp. 353–80). London: Sage.

Le Fanu, J. (1999). *The rise and fall of modern medicine.* New York: Carroll & Graf.

Letzing, J., & Lublin, J. (2011, September 8). Yahoo's "numbers guy" takes lead, for now. *Wall Street Journal*, B4.

Levin, H. M. (2009). The economic payoff to investing in educational justice. *Educational Researcher, 38*(1), 5–20. doi:10.3102/0013189X08331192.

Logan, J. (1999, Summer). An educational leadership challenge: Refocusing gender equity strategies. *AASA Professor.* Arlington, VA: AASA.

Lortie, D. (1969). The balance of control and autonomy in elementary school teaching. In A. Etzioni (Ed.), *The semi-professions and their organization* (pp. 1–53). New York: Free Press.

Marshall, C., & Oliva, M. (2010). *Leadership for social justice: Making revolutions in education* (2nd ed.). Boston: Allyn & Bacon.

Martin, T. (2011, July 13). Atlanta school scandal sparks house cleaning. *Wall Street Journal*, A3.

Martinez, B., & Saul, M. (2011, April 8). Black eye for Bloomberg. *Wall Street Journal*, A3.

McCarthy, M. M., & Kuh, G. D. (1997). *Continuity and change: The educational leadership professoriate*. Columbia, MO: University Council for Educational Administration.

Mead, W. (2011, March/April). The Tea Party and American foreign policy: What populism means for globalism. *Foreign Affairs, 90*(2), 28–44.

Melendez de Santa Ana, T. (2011, March). Bold ideas for secondary school reform. *Principal Leadership, 11*(7), 23–26.

Middleton, D. (2010a). Harvard Business School names Nohria new dean. *Wall Street Journal*, B9.

Middleton, D. (2010b). B-schools try makeover. *Wall Street Journal*, B5.

Miron, G. (2010, February). Escalating evidence on charter segregation. Education and the Public Interest Center, School of Education, University of Colorado at Boulder. Retrieved February 24, 2010, from http://epicpolicy.org/publication/schools-without-diversity.

Mountain Dreamer, O. (2004). *Opening the invitation.* New York: Harper.

Morris, I. (2010). *Why the West rules—for now: The patterns of history, and what they reveal about the future.* New York: Farrar, Straus & Giroux.

Mullen, C. (2011). The paradox of change in public schooling and educational leadership. In F. English (Ed.), *The SAGE handbook of educational leadership: Advances in theory, research, and practice* (2nd ed.). Thousand Oaks, CA: Sage.

Mullen, C. A. (2010). 21st-century priorities for leadership education and prospective school leaders. *Scholar-Practitioner Quarterly, 4*(4), 331–33.

Mullen, C. A. (Ed.). (2009). *The handbook of leadership and professional learning communities*. New York: Palgrave Macmillan.

Murphy, J. (1992). *The landscape of leadership preparation*. Newbury Park, CA: Corwin.

Murphy, J., Moorman, H., & McCarthy, M. (2008). A framework for rebuilding initial certification and preparation programs in educational leadership: Lessons from whole-state reform initiatives. *Teachers College Record, 110*(10), 2172–203.

Nasser, H. E. (2008, February 12). U.S. Hispanic population to triple by 2050. *USA Today*. Retrieved March 12, 2011, from www.usatoday.com/news/nation/2008-02-11-population-study_N.htm.

National Center for Education Statistics. (2011). *Characteristics of school principals*. Retrieved October 12, 2011, from www.education.com/print/Ref_School_Principals.

National Policy Center. (2006). *Poverty in the United States*. Retrieved March 6, 2011, from http://npc.umich.edu/poverty.

National Research Council. (2002). *Scientific research in education*. Washington, DC: National Academy Press.

Nisbet, R. (1980). *History of the idea of progress.* New York: Basic Books.

Orfield, G., & Lee, C. (2007). *Historic reversals, accelerating resegregation, and the need for new integration strategies* (pp. 1–49) [A report of the Civil Rights Project, UCLA]. Retrieved March 9, 2011, from http://civilrightsproject.ucla.edu/.

Ortiz, F., & Marshall, C. (1988). Women in educational administration. In N. Boyan (Ed.), *Handbook of research on educational administration* (pp. 123–57). New York: Longman.

Papa, R. (Ed.). (2011a). *Technology leadership for school improvement.* Thousand Oaks, CA: Sage.

Papa, R. (2011b). Standards for educational leaders: Promises, paradoxes, and pitfalls. In F. English (Ed.), *The SAGE handbook of educational leadership: Advances in theory, research, and practice* (2nd ed., pp. 195–209). Thousand Oaks, CA: Sage.

Papa, R., & English, F. W. (2011). *Turnaround principals for underperforming schools.* Lanham, MD: Rowman & Littlefield.

Papa, R., & English, F. (2010). Part 2: The good, the bad, and the ugly: A critical review of trends in dissertation research in educational leadership, 2006–08. In F. English & R. Papa, *Restoring human agency to educational administration: Status and strategies* (pp. 47–75). Lancaster, PA: Pro-Active.

Papa [a.k.a. Papa-Lewis], R., & Fortune, R. (2002). *Leadership on purpose: Promising practices for African American and Hispanic students.* Thousand Oaks, CA: Corwin.

Papa, R., & Papa, J. (2011). Leading adult learners: Preparing future leaders and professional development of those they lead. In R. Papa (Ed.), *Technology leadership for school improvement.* Thousand Oaks, CA: Sage.

Peck, C. M., Mullen, C. A., Lashley, C., & Eldridge, J. A. (2011). School leadership and technology challenges: Lessons from a new American high school. *AASA Journal of Scholarship and Practice, 7*(4), 39–51. Retrieved March 8, 2011, from www.aasa.org/uploadedFiles/Publications/Newsletters/JSP_Winter2011.Final.pdf.

Peterson, E., & Posner, R. (2010, January). The world's water challenge. *Current History, 109*(723), 31–34.

Popkin, S. J., Acs, G., & Smith, R. E. (2010). *The urban institute's program on neighborhoods and youth development: Understanding how place matters for kids.* Retrieved March 6, 2011, from www.urban.org/publications/411974.htm.

Popper, K. (1965). *Conjectures and refutations: The growth of scientific knowledge.* New York: Harper & Row.

Portner, H., & Portner, M. H. (in press). Using best practices for teaching the process of coaching. In S. Fletcher & C. A. Mullen (Eds.), *The SAGE handbook of mentoring and coaching in education.* Thousand Oaks, CA: Sage.

Powell, D. (2011, August 24). Finding hope in Atlanta. *Education Week, 31*(1), 25, 30.

The Profession: Colleges' reliance on part-time and nontenured faculty has grown. (2011). *Chronicle of Higher Education, 53*(1), 28.

Pugh, T. (2011, September 8). 1 in 6 in U.S. deal with "food insecurity." Raleigh *News and Observer*, 7A.

Quillen, I. (2011, August 10). Scandal clouds News Corp.'s move into education. *Education Week, 30*(37), 1, 18.

Rawls, J. (1971). *A theory of justice.* Cambridge, MA: Harvard University Press.

Reddy, S. (2011, March 25). Latinos fuel growth in decade. *Wall Street Journal*, A2.

Rhee, M. (2011, January 11). In budget crises, an opening for school reform. *Wall Street Journal*, A17.

Rhee, M., & Fenty, A. (2010, October 30–31). The education manifesto. *Wall Street Journal*, C1–2.

Rhodes, R. (1994). The hollowing out of the state: Changing the nature of the public service in Britain. *Political Quarterly, 65*(2), 138–51.

Riley, J. (2011, March 26–27). Weingarten for the union defense. *Wall Street Journal*, A13.

Riley, N. (2009, August 29–30). We're in the venture philanthrophy business. *Wall Street Journal*, A11.

Rotberg, I. (2011, September 14). International test scores, irrelevant policies. *Education Week, 31*(3), 32.

Russett, B. (2010, January). Peace in the twenty-first century? *Current History, 109*(723), 11–16.

Samuels, C. A. (2011, February 9). Survey detects shifting priorities of school boards. *Education Week, 30*(20), 1, 22.

Schachter, R. (2010). A call for technology leadership. *District Administration, 46*(10), 41–45. Retrieved March 8, 2011, from www.districtadministration.com.

Schally, P. (2006). Curiosity does not kill the cat. *Leader's Almanac.* Retrieved April 9, 2011, from http://sonomaleadership.com/newsletter/06-winter.

Schmidt, E., & Cohen, J. (2010, November–December). The digital disruption: Connectivity and diffusion of power. *Foreign Affairs, 89*(6), 75–85.

Schrader, P. (2008). Learning in technology: Reconceptualizing immersive environments. *AACE Journal, 16*, 457–75.

Schultz, R., & Dew, A. (2006). *Insurgents, terrorists and militias: The warriors of contemporary combat.* New York: Columbia University Press.

Schuster, J., & Finkelstein, M. (2006). *The American faculty: The restructuring of academic and work and careers.* Baltimore: Johns Hopkins University Press.

Schwarz, A. (2011, July 12). Union chief faults school reform from "on high." *New York Times*, A11.

Severson, K. (2011, September 8). The icon, the scandal and the fall from grace. *New York Times*, A16.

Shakeshaft, C. (2011). Wild patience: Women in school administration. In F. English (Ed.), *The SAGE handbook of educational leadership* (2nd ed., pp. 210–22). Thousand Oaks, CA: Sage.

Shakeshaft, C. (1993). Gender equity in schools. In C. Capper (Ed.), *Educational administration in a pluralistic society* (pp. 86–109). Albany: SUNY Press.

Simmons, W. (2010, Winter). Urban education reform: Recalibrating the federal rule. *Voices in Urban Reform, 26*, 54–64.

Sirin, S. (2005, Fall). Socioeconomic status and academic achievement: A meta-analytic review of research. *Review of Educational Research, 75*(3), 417–53.

Sparks, S. (2011, July 13). 2-Year Hispanic academic gaps persist in math, reading. *Education Week, 30*(36), 14.

Spence, M. (2011, July/August). The impact of globalization on income and employment: The downside of integrating markets. *Foreign Affairs, 90*(4), 28–41.

Spillane, J. P., Halverson, R., & Diamond, J. B. (2004). Towards a theory of leadership practice: A distributed perspective. *Journal of Curriculum Studies, 36*(1), 3–34.

Spillane, J., Halverson, R., & Diamond, J. (2001). Investigation school leadership practice: A distributed perspective. *Educational Researcher, 30*(3), 23–28.

Spring, J. (2010). *Political agendas for education* (4th ed.). New York: Routledge.

Springer, M., Ballou, D., Hamilton, L., Vi-Nhuan, L., Lockwood, J., McCaffrey, D., Pepper, M., & Stecher, B. (2010, September 21). *Teacher pay for performance: Experimental evidence from the project on Incentives in Teaching.* National Center for Incentives in Teaching. Vanderbilt University and the University of Missouri and the Rand Corporation.

Starbuck, W., & Milliken, F. (1988). Executives' perceptual filters: What they notice and how they make sense. In D. Hambrick (Ed.), *The executive effect: Concepts and methods for studying top managers* (pp. 35–65). Greenwick, CT: JAI.

Sterne, J. (2003). Bourdieu, technique and technology. *Cultural Studies, 17*(3/4), 367–89.

Stiglitz, J. (2010). *Freefall: America, free markets, and the sinking of the world economy.* New York: Norton.

Student demographics: Colleges awarding the most doctorates, by selected disciplines, 2008–9. (2011). *Chronicle of Higher Education, 53*(1), 40.

Sweig, J. (2010, November–December). A new global player. *Foreign Affairs, 89*(6), 173–85.

Tapsott, D. (2009). *Grown up digital: How the Net Generation is changing your world.* New York: McGraw-Hill.

ThinkExist. (1999–2010). *Seneca quotes.* Retrieved May 2, 2011, from http://thinkexist.com/quotation/its_not_because_things_are_difficult_that_we/214305.html.

Thomas B. Fordham Institute & Broad Foundation. (2003). *Better leaders for America's schools: A manifesto.* Retrieved February 11, 2004, from www.edexcellencemedia.net/publications/2003/200305_betterleaders/manifesto.pdf.

Tirozzi, G. N. (2011, April). Alternate paths to the principalship . . . for some other kid's school: Message from the executive director. *Newsleader, 58*(8), 2.

Tyack, D. B. (1974). *The one best system.* Cambridge, MA: Harvard University Press.

Umphrey, J. (2011, March). A time for resolve: A conversation with Diane Ravitch. *Principal Leadership, 11*(7), 34–36.

Useem, J. (2003, April 28). Have they no shame? *Fortune, 147*(8), 56–58.

Wacquant, L. (1992). Toward a social praxeology: The structure and logic of Bourdieu's sociology. In P. Bourdieu & L. Wacquant (Eds.), *An invitation to reflexive sociology* (pp. 7–47). Chicago: University of Chicago Press.

Webster's seventh new collegiate dictionary. (1971). s.v. conjecture. Springfield, MA: G. & C. Merriam.

Weick, K. (1998). *Sensemaking in organizations.* Thousand Oaks, CA: Sage.

West, P. T., Piper, D., Achilles, C. M., & Manley, C. A. (1988). *The 4th decade of NCPEA: 1977–1986.* National Council of Professors of Educational Administration: University of North Dakota Press.

Whyte, W. H. (1956). *The organization man.* New York: Simon & Schuster.

Wilson, S., Rozelle, J., & Mikeska, J. (2011, September/October). Cacophony or embarrassment of riches? Building a system of support for quality teaching. *Journal of Teacher Education, 62*(4), 383–94.

Winston, C., & Crandall, R. (2011, August 22). Time to deregulate the practice of law. *Wall Street Journal*, A13.

Wood, G. H. (2011, March). The future of education: A look at what has and hasn't happened in education reveals hope for the future. *Principal Leadership, 11*(7), 19–21.

Woods, P. (2005). *Democratic leadership in education.* London: Paul Chapman.

World Bank. (2005). *What is poverty?* Retrieved March 10, 2011, from http://web.worldbank.org/wbsite/external/topics/extpoverty/0,contentMDK:22569747~pagePK:148956~piPK:216618~theSitePK:336992,00.html.

York-Barr, J., & Duke, K. (2004, Fall). What do we know about teacher leadership? Findings from two decades of scholarship. *Review of Educational Research, 74*(3), 255–316.

Index

Meet the Coauthors and NCPEA

This special report was completed by a special task force of the National Council of Professors of Educational Administration (NCPEA), the oldest organization of professors of educational administration in the United States. It does not represent any official position or perspective of NCPEA, but rather is inclusive of a wide range of perspectives that comprise the membership. It was written to provoke and promote viewpoints that the authors consider crucial to the future of the profession itself.

The authors of this report are scholar-practitioners and included the following:

- Three former school superintendents and two mid-level administrators
- Current NCPEA executive director
- All former and/or current NCPEA board members
- Current president (2012) and president-elect (2013)
- Current chair of NCPEA Publications Executive Committee
- Current NCPEA director of publications
- Former NCPEA executive director (2001–2006)
- Two former NCPEA presidents (1992 and 1999)
- One former UCEA president (2006)

- One participant in the formation of the National Policy Board for Educational Administration who served as an original member (1991–1993)
- Current member of the NPBEA
- Former member of the NPBEA (2001–2006)

SO WHO ARE THE SCHOLAR-PRACTITIONERS?

NCPEA considers itself an organization of scholar-practitioners. A large number of the members are former school teachers and administrators who have learned the ins and outs of the challenges of leadership by living them on a day-to-day basis. They have put in their time both inside and outside of classrooms and schools; been responsive to state departments of education, federal mandates, school board dictates and elections; and collectively bargained with teacher and other employee unions and associations. Schools and classrooms are not abstractions to them or easily classified or topologized.

Our members have worked both for and against the policies and politics of local American education. We understand that such experiences do not always convey wisdom, but they do provide our teaching with a certain kind of contextual richness and understanding of complexity that defy simple bromides for improvement and change. They are also the wellspring of a certain kind of professional skepticism about social do-gooders, policy wonks, think tank pundits, and legislative remedies that lack any real understanding of the day-to-day realities of school work.

In short, we believe for real change to become a reality in the schools, change proposals have to be embedded in the nuances of the work that actually goes on in them. Randi Weingarten, president of the American Federation of Teachers, said it most trenchantly: "Let's refuse to be defined by people who are happy to lecture us about the state of public education—but wouldn't last 10 minutes in a classroom" (Schwarz, 2011, p. A11).

Similarly, we could add, "Let's refuse to be defined by critics and reformers who have not walked the line of keeping schools good places for children while balancing competing interests, conflicting demands, and managing the enterprise with declining resources." And we would also say, "Let's refuse to be captured by special interests who want to use the schools to make money and that impose accountability models that destroy democracy and community along with the ethic of public service."

So a scholar-practitioner is one who approaches teaching, research, and service from a "real-time" as opposed to "virtual-time" or "case-study-time" perspective. A scholar-practitioner is respectful of theory, understands that practice is anchored in theory, but approaches problem solving from "what works" rather than constructing new theories first and then sorting out the problems to be solved. A "practice first" approach is what has enabled some of the most spectacular discoveries in medicine (another practical field) to be made because nearly all of them were "out of paradigm" or "out of theory" at the time (Le Fanu, 1999).

We like this definition of the work of a scholar-practitioner:

> This holistic practice-based approach integrates academic knowledge of theory, pedagogy, and curriculum across experiences in authentic contexts that are embedded in focused inquiry, directed observation, and guided practice. (Hollins, 2011, p. 395)

The universities and colleges we work in are research intensive, doctoral research and master's, public and private institutions. We represent the broadest range of higher education institutions in the nation.

THE SCHOLAR-PRACTITIONER COAUTHORS OF THIS SPECIAL REPORT

Fenwick W. English

Fenwick W. English is currently the R. Wendell Eaves Senior Professor of Educational Leadership in the School of Education at the University of North Carolina at Chapel Hill, a position he has held since 2001. Fen is a former public school elementary and middle school teacher; middle school assistant principal and principal in California; assistant superintendent of schools in Florida; and superintendent of schools in New York. He also served as associate executive director of the AASA and a partner in the consulting and accounting firm of Peat, Marwick & Mitchell in Washington, DC.

In academic administration, he has been a department chair, dean, and vice chancellor of academic affairs at universities in Ohio and Indiana. He is the author or coauthor of more than thirty books in education and more than one hundred journal articles, including publications in *Educational Researcher*; *Educational Administration Quarterly*; *Journal of School Leadership*; *International Journal of Leadership in Education: Theory and Practice*; *Educational Policy*; *Leadership and Policy in Schools*; *Journal of Educational Administration and History*; *Journal of Educational Administration*; and *Studies in Philosophy and Education*.

He served as the editor of the 2006 *SAGE Encyclopedia of Educational Leadership and Administration* (two volumes); editor of the 2009 *SAGE Library of Educational Thought and Practice: Educational Leadership and Administration* (four volumes); and editor of the 2011 *SAGE Handbook of Educational Leadership* (second edition). He is the current president of NCPEA (2011–2012) and former president of UCEA (2006–2007). His PhD was earned in 1972 at Arizona State University.

Rosemary Papa

Rosemary Papa holds the Del and Jewel Lewis Endowed Chair in Learning Centered Leadership and is professor of Educational Leadership in the College of Education at Northern Arizona University, a position she has held since 2007. Her practitioner experiences include serving as a school principal and chief school administrator of schools in Nebraska.

Her academic administrative experience includes assistant vice chancellor for academic affairs and faculty director of a university-based center for teaching and learning in California and founder of two joint doctoral programs in educational leadership with the University of California. She has worked internationally in China, Korea, and West Africa. She was the first female president of NCPEA (1991–1992) and recipient of the 2003 NCPEA Living Legend Award.

She was also honored to give the Walter Cocking lecture both in 1999 and in 2011. In addition, she served as president of the Arizona Professors of Education Administration (2008–2010) and president of the California Professors of Educational Administration (1989–1990). In 2000 she founded and currently serves as editor of the *JEP* (*Journal of Education Policy*), one of the first open-access, free, blind peer-reviewed journals in the world.

Her record of publications includes ten books, numerous book chapters, monographs, and over eighty referred journal articles. Her 2011 book with coauthor Fenwick English is titled *Turnaround Principals for Underperforming Schools*. She earned her EdD at the University of Nebraska, Lincoln, in 1983.

Carol A. Mullen

Carol A. Mullen is professor and chair of educational leadership in the School of Education at the University of North Carolina at Greensboro, having been in this position since 2007. She specializes in mentoring, diversity, and innovations in learning and professional development within the leadership field across higher education and K–12 settings, and she mentors new professionals and collaborates with scholars and practitioners.

Carol has taught in universities and colleges in the United States and Canada since 1985. She teaches doctoral courses that include scholarly writing. She was editor of the *Mentoring & Tutoring: Partnership in Learning* journal (Routledge). Her authorships encompass more than two hundred refereed journal articles and book chapters, fourteen special issues of journals, and fourteen books. Edited books include *The SAGE Handbook of Mentoring and Coaching in Education* (forthcoming in 2012).

Awards received include AERA's Award for *Breaking the Circle of One* from Division K; the USF President's Award for Faculty Excellence and Women's Leadership Award; and the Florida Association for Supervision and Curriculum Development's Excellence in Teaching and Research Award. In 1997, she founded AERA's special interest group Mentorship and Mentoring Practices. In 1999, she also established AERA's mentoring for academic writing program. She founded USF's new faculty mentoring program and served as the director.

Carol is president-elect of NCPEA and will serve her term in 2012–2013. She is also a UCEA plenary session representative. She earned her PhD in 1994 from the Ontario Institute for Studies in Education of the University of Toronto.

Theodore Creighton

Ted Creighton is currently director of publications for NCPEA. Formerly he was professor at Idaho State University, Sam Houston State University (where he served as director of doctoral programs in educational leadership), and most recently (2006–2011) program leader of educational leadership at Virginia Tech. From 2000 to 2005, he served as executive director of the National Council of

Professors of Educational Administration and, during those years, as a member of the National Policy Board for Educational Administration.

He was instrumental as the coordinator of the Carnegie Project on the Educational Doctorate (CPED) in helping to reform the educational leadership programs at Virginia Tech. His practitioner experience includes teaching for the Cleveland public schools and Los Angeles Unified School District and serving as principal and superintendent of schools in both Fresno and Kern Counties, California. Presently, Creighton edits the *International Journal of Educational Leadership Preparation (IJELP)* and *Education Leadership Review (ELR)* and directs the NCPEA/Connexions Project. Creighton has authored twelve books, including the seminal *Schools and Data: The Educator's Guide to Using Data to Improve Decision Making.*

James Berry, Executive Director of NCPEA

James Berry is a professor of educational administration in the Department of Leadership & Counseling at Eastern Michigan University. Dr. Berry began his K–12 career in upstate New York as a high school English teacher and has held positions as elementary principal, assistant high school principal, and assistant superintendent.

His career in higher education began in 1991 at Eastern Michigan University. He was actively involved in developing Eastern Michigan University's first campus doctoral program (educational administration) and went on to serve as a department head and associate dean for the college. He has been active in the National Council of Professors of Educational Administration (NCPEA), having served on the executive board from 2000 to 2003. He currently serves as executive director of NCPEA.

He also currently serves as board chair for the Connexions Consortium, which is a long-term initiative to create an open source database on the Internet. He has conducted research and written articles in the area of K–12 school reform with a focus on change leadership and the use of technology.

He was actively involved in drafting guidelines for the implementation of administrative standards in Michigan and served as a member of a Michigan Department of Education committee to implement university-based certification for K–12 administrators. He has served as a Michigan state and NCATE reviewer for the accreditation of programs in educational administration.

A BRIEF HISTORY OF THE NCPEA

The First Decade of NCPEA: 1947–1956

In 1947, charter members of NCPEA came together in Atlantic City, New Jersey, to discuss their mutual interests in the theory and practice of educational administration. This prearranged meeting included fifty-six men. Walter D. Cocking, then editor of *The School Executive*, and E. B. Norton, professor of educational administration at Teachers College, Columbia University, took leadership roles in planning this two-hour meeting. Walter Dewey Cocking was the founder of NCPEA.

It was Walter Cocking who secured the "Homestead," the country club of the IBM Corporation in Endicott, New York, at no cost for a ten-day meeting. This first meeting, with Julian Butterworth from Cornell University as its chair, was attended by seventy-two professional persons, the majority representing colleges and universities.

The objectives of the conference were to "achieve among conference members a better understanding of the problems of developing leaders in education" and to bring about "a common approach regarding the methods and techniques for the more effective preparation of educational administrators" (West, Piper, Achilles, & Manley, 1988).

In the years to follow, annual meetings were held at the University of Wisconsin (1948) with fifty-six participants; Cornell University in 1950 with 120 professors; Greeley, Colorado, in 1951; Penn State in 1952; East Lansing in 1953; Denver in 1954; Storrs, Connecticut, in 1955; and Fayetteville, Arkansas, in 1956. This first decade was a period of actual survival and growth. NCPEA began to open its sessions to outsiders, and NCPEA professors moved their attention from mere techniques and practices toward a theory of administration.

The founding fathers of NCPEA established a "key legacy" that has continued to be at the foundation of NCPEA for over sixty-four years: *"Enticing professors of educational administration out of their self-contained worlds into cooperative ventures with their colleagues."*

The Second Decade: 1957–1966

The issues at the annual meeting in 1959 were multiple and complex but, for the most part, centered on the concerns of local versus state and/or national control and finance. As the decade progressed, the impact of that thrust became apparent because new types of administrators were needed. Special "whither NCPEA meetings" were called in this decade in 1958, 1959, 1963, 1965, 1966, and 1969 to consider the goals, success, future, and current needs of NCPEA.

This second decade of NCPEA emphasized the following areas: an assessment of NCPEA's direction, the behavioral sciences and administrative theory, development of a recurring cycle of program emphasis, institutionalization of some aspects of the annual conferences, a look at the future, and publication.

The Third Decade: 1967–1976

In 1967, NCPEA marked the beginning of its third decade with the establishment of the Walter D. Cocking Lectures in Educational Administration, a lecture series designed to provide an opportunity for an annual presentation of a very important and influential paper in the field of educational administration. The ten lecturers during this decade included leaders in educational administration; authorities in the fields of political science, sociology, and planning; and leading proponents for urban, social, and educational concerns.

In 1973, the Edgar L. Morphet Fund was established to support appropriate projects or activities associated with the annual NCPEA conference. Today, the Morphet Award is targeted toward the highest kind of scholarship in the field of educational administration: doctoral dissertations. Each year NCPEA presents the Outstanding Dissertation Award.

In 1976, at the Knoxville conference, cohosts John Hoyle and Chuck Achilles made the first recorded focus on women professors and education leaders (personal communication, March 2007) with a featured general session titled "Women as Leaders." The glass ceiling began to crack for NCPEA in 1976, and giant strides have been made today with an open door for women and members of color.

The Fourth Decade: 1977–1986

The fourth decade was characterized by a membership becoming restless and searching for new direction and purpose. NCPEA's name was changed from the National *Conference* of Professors of Educational Administration to the National *Council* of Professors of Educational Administration. The planning committee became the executive board, and the position of planning committee chair became the president of the executive board. After thirty-eight years of no membership dues or fees, in 1985 the executive board approved a $10 membership fee that would be added to the conference registration.

More attention and concern emerged around politics, policy, and economics; the *real world* and international issues; and effective schooling and excellence. But underlying the shifting concerns remained the solid purpose of improving the profession, the practice of educational administration, and the preparation of administrators.

The Fifth Decade: 1987–1996

Of extreme significance during the fifth decade was attention to diversity. For nearly forty years, NCPEA members and conference attendees were, for the most part, white men. Few women other than spouses were in attendance, even up to the 1987 Chadron, Nebraska, conference (Papa, personal communication, 2011).

A woman professor named Rosemary Papa (a.k.a. Papa-Lewis) would be elected to the executive board that year and become the board president in 1992. The glass ceiling began to shatter, with women presidents Paula Short (1994), Maria Shelton (1995), Cheryl Fisher (1999), Judith Adkison (2001), Elaine Wilmore (2003), and Linda Morford (2007).

The Sixth Decade: 1997–2006

Arriving in 1996 as a new and very able executive director, Robert Beach not only brought fiscal responsibility and solvency to NCPEA but also represented NCPEA on the National Policy Board of Educational Administration. This provided a voice at the table with nine other professional organizations and for the first time gave NCPEA an opportunity to really address "politics, policy, and economics" and provide input on such things as national standards for the preparation of educational leaders came to the surface. His five years solidified the financial base and organizational structure of NCPEA.

Beach also laid the foundation with the board to prepare for some very significant and perhaps radical roads ahead. The NCPEA executive board was about to hear proposals to (1) increase its presence and awareness via a dynamic website; (2) implement online conference registrations and payments; (3) hold fall strategic planning retreats; and (4) enter collaborative ventures with other professional organizations such as NASSP, NAESP, AASA, and UCEA, with three of these organizations sending representatives to become affiliate executive board members.

In 2004, NCPEA initiated a collaborative venture with Rice University called the NCPEA Connexions Knowledge Base Project. The purpose of this project was to begin to assemble/publish the Educational Administration Knowledge Base in one central location, free and open to all across the globe, especially professors, students, and practitioners in the field. In 2005, NCPEA began to focus on its scholarly publications: *The NCPEA Yearbook* and *Education Leadership Review*.

Both publications retained nationally recognized editors and gained the status of peer-reviewed Tier I publications. In 2006, the Connexions Project expanded to the creation of NCPEA Press—an on-demand printing process that allowed students and professors anywhere in the world to order high-quality hardback textbooks from Connexions, in most cases for less than $25.

THE NCPEA TODAY

To continue, we organize this section around five areas: (1) individual and institutional membership, (2) collaborative efforts and initiatives with other professional organizations, (3) programs served, (4) values added, and (5) information on the authors.

Individual, Institutional Membership, and State Affiliates

NCPEA currently has over four hundred active members representing approximately 250 universities and/or school districts. Universities include public, private, and for-profit institutions. Membership is all inclusive; the only requirement is that the prospective member be (1) a member of higher education faculty (active or retired) assisting in the preparation of school leaders, (2) a district and site-based school practitioner with an interest in educational administration, and/or (3) a doctoral student in educational leadership areas of study.

Membership is not dependent on the status of the university, the credentials of the member, or other limiting bias or discriminating factors. Presently, NCPEA membership is diverse racially, with members who are male, female, gay, lesbian, bisexual, and transgendered academics from fourteen countries, including China, Japan, Australia, New Zealand, Saudi Arabia, Canada, Great Britain, and Russia.

In addition to individual membership, NCPEA solicits and accepts institutional membership, where an institution (university) submits its department or program faculty members for NCPEA membership. Institutional members receive reduced rates, along with free subscriptions to NCPEA publications. As with individual membership, institutional membership does not use university status or other requirements for admission.

Very significant are the numbers of NCPEA state affiliate members, bringing state associations into the NCPEA circle of professional development and contributions to the scholarship and practice of educational administration.

Collaboration with AASA, NAESP, NASSP, and UCEA

NCPEA has representatives from AASA, NASSP, and NAESP serving as affiliate executive board members. We are the only national professorial organization that sits with practitioner organizations as partners at our executive board level.

Our midwinter conference-within-a-conference is held at the aforementioned organization's annual conference on a rotating basis. Since 1991, there have been strong collaborative relations and initiatives between NCPEA and the University Council of Educational Administration (UCEA).

Research and Publication

NCPEA strives to offers its members (individual and institutional) many benefits and opportunities for professional development and growth. Here are just a few:

- Free and open access to the Knowledge Base in Educational Administration
- Low membership rates (i.e., $150 per year)
- Publishing opportunities

  - *Education Leadership Review* (our premier peer-reviewed journal)
  - *NCPEA Yearbook* (published each year for the annual conference)
  - *International Journal of Educational Leadership Preparation* (official peer-reviewed electronic journal of the NCPEA Connexions Project)
  - *Mentoring and Tutoring: Partnership in Learning* (sponsored by NCPEA and published by Routledge)
  - Online access to NCPEA Press, Open Education Resources (which has 1,500 visits per month, averaging fifty per day, from sixty-two countries and territories and all fifty US states)

- Opportunity for an on-demand printing process for members that allows students and professors anywhere in the world to order high-quality hardback textbooks from Connexions, in most cases for less than $25

- Open forum for conversation about educational leadership issues and pressing problems, political and social commentary, new publications, and more (via the NCPEA blog with Facebook and Twitter support)
- Opportunity to serve as publication editors and reviewers (currently over five hundred strong)
- Individual author tracking data provided through Google Analytics and Connexions Statistics (upon request, these data are supplied to members for tenure and promotion needs)
- NCPEA Mosaic Mentoring Program, establishing relationships in which mentors provide assistance to other members in the areas of teaching, research, and/or service